Frie

Pet Health Articles

By "Dr. Bob" Zepecki, DVM

To his family + Bear

Dr. Bob

Woof! Woof!

"Dr. Bob" Zepecki, DVM
Published by Avery Anne Publishers
www.averyannepublishers.com

Library of Congress
LC control no.: 2014946034

ISBN-13: 978-0692254653
ISBN-10: 069225465X

CONTENTS

Prologue...5

Introduction...7

Chapter One...9

   The "First Article" and Welcome......................9

Chapter Two...12

   A New Friend..12

Chapter Three..14

   New Year's Resolutions from the Past...........14

Chapter 4..20

   Your Friend's Body...20

Chapter 5..51

   Some Common Medical Problems.................51

Chapter 6..76

   Allergies in Arkansas and the Midsouth.........76

Chapter 7..83

   Emergency First Aid at Home........................83

Chapter 8..88

   Nutrition...88

Chapter 9..90

   Silver Seniors...90

Chapter 10..105

   Wellness and Good Health............................105

Chapter 11..120

   "Buggy" Articles for the...............................120

   Village and Surrounding Areas.....................120

Chapter 12..134

   Disaster Preparedness for the Village...........134

Chapter 13..139

   Friends and Neighbors in Passing.................139

"Dr. Bob" Zepecki, DVM

Prologue

"Dr. Bob", as he is known to his clients in Hot Springs Village, Arkansas, has been in the continuous practice of veterinary medicine since 1973. During these many years he has treated and cared for the Animal Kingdom from mice to African Lions, from sparrows to macaws, and just about everything in between!! His practice experience extends from the tropical city of Ft. Lauderdale, to Illinois, southern Missouri, and Arkansas. "Dr. Bob" practiced in rural Arkansas for fifteen years before coming to Hot Springs Village, a retirement paradise located in the Ouachita Mountains north of Hot Springs, Arkansas. Dr. Bob was entirely pleased by the attention and care that Villager pets (we call them Friends) receive from their parents. This human-animal bond is a significant part of the life and health of this Village community and continually demonstrates that people that are kind to animals are kind to each other. In 1998, In the course of his practice experience in Hot Springs Village, "Dr. Bob" began writing for the LaVilla newspaper. The warm and enthusiastic response to these articles by his many readers has led to the consolidation and publication of this book. It is his hope that each reader will find some answers to questions. After all, having the responsibility of a "Friend" (dog or cat) does require an informed human!

The articles contained in this book are presented in an order that should be easier to follow.

The LaVilla format is used where still appropriate. I have expanded and altered some of the original articles to more fully explain or simply update the topics.

Introduction

I was sitting in front of my computer in Corning, Arkansas , trying to decide what to do about practice and my life in general, when I noticed the AVMA Journal (the professional journal for veterinarians) open to the job classifications. There was an opening for an associate in Arkansas in the AVMA Journal, which was not a frequent occurrence. That opening was in Hot Springs Village, Arkansas. I had actually passed through Hot Springs Village, Arkansas in 1978 and decided not to open a practice there at that time due to the small population of the Village. Despite the enthusiasm of the Razorback Realty agent, I was not sure that this small community, with mostly gravel roads and big ideas would eventually blossom into this lovely retirement community with all of the services of a self-contained, self-governed community. I was particularly impressed by the close relationships between "Villagers" and their pets. That is why I began calling the doggies and kitty cats here "Friends", because that is what they are to Villagers. I first practiced at the Village Pet Clinic in the Village. Twenty-five years of solo practice experience resulted in a reevaluation of my practice philosophy which led me back to my roots in a House Call practice, or "Home Practice", as I like to call it. The immediate success of this in-home service and the need for hospitalization and observation of aged or ill pets resulted in the creation of the Village Animal Group. I am currently planning a complete spa resort so that Villagers and their Friends will have the first class treatment they deserve at their front door. I am calling this book Friends and Neighbors because that is what you and your pets are to me!! Dr. Bob

Chapter One

The "First Article" and Welcome

Greetings and Salutations!!!!

Greetings from Paradise! As this is my first article with the kind permission and enthusiastic endorsement of all creatures great and small, and the LaVilla staff and editor, I thought I would preview for you the direction and scope of my articles on pets (or as we know them, Friends). The Village is really a dream come true for many of you as it is for me. I have traveled to many parts of the world, and have not seen any region comparable to this location. This is a great place for both your and your Friends to enjoy. We are perched on top of a mountain in the northern part of the Gulf of Mexico climate. This particular latitude provides a favorable climate for approximately 150 more varieties of plants and shrubs and flowers than can grow in northeast Arkansas a mere 170 miles north from here. Many of these plants, shrubs and flowers are native to this area. Of course, this wild group also contains the poison oak/sumac/ivy type of climbing plants that are basically here for ten months of the year. They are a cause for concern for you and you're Friends. You should familiarize yourself with these plants and be able to recognize them and avoid them if you can. The benefit of being on top of this mountain does reduce some of the harsher aspects of this warm climate in that we have a lot of shade. The green belts here temper the heat. And the hilltops provide a ready supply of breezes. Having lived in the Arkansas Delta for the past fifteen years, I can tell you that you and your friends have the best in climate that Arkansas can offer.

Please remember that our wild friends have occupied these mountains and valleys for many generations. Some slither, and some slink, and some consider your Friends as dinner. The wild friends recognized what a great place this is. So we must learn to live with them. If you leave food outside, don't be surprised if they come and visit you, a lot! The predators that feed on the small creatures that come to visit you will also start spending some time around your premises. So watch your Friends closely or please stop leaving food outside.

We are blessed with ten months of warm, lovely weather. This type of weather is easy on the joints and permits many activities for both us and our Friends. As you have all discovered in one manner or another, the insect portion of our environment likes it here....a lot! The only basic difference in dealing with these insect residents of the Village is that you will have to do the same things here that you did in your previous locations for your Friends, but more often. I will deal with insects and skin conditions in another article as these are the most prevalent problems presented at the clinic. It is my observation that you have all worked very hard for a lot of years to get here. In other words, you have earned your way here. I am continually impressed by the intellect, talent, and capabilities of the Villagers I have met. I know that you are all intelligent because you laugh at my jokes! You deserve to enjoy yourselves here and have a nice life. I will do what I can to give your Friends some portion of that same enjoyment through good health. Many of them are retired also! They have given unconditional love to you and probably helped you raise a child or two. They will continue to give you their unfailing loyalty and attention. But they will age faster than you will. They are fortunate that you now have the time to give some attention and care back in that way to them.

Chapter Two

A New Friend

A New Friend: An Affair Of The Heart

We all moved here for our own reasons; and most brought along our friends. We arrived here, in various degrees of anticipation, with mixed feelings of apprehension, relief, and excitement. Our friends wondered what this was all about, but came with us anyway. Just being with us was enough for them. Many friends were old before the Village time in their lives. Adjusting was difficult. New smells to be savored. Hills and more hills. Our city friends were surprised and likely pleased at the sight of all of those trees... and critters. Squirrels, chipmunks, you name it, they chased it. So much quality time with mom and pop. And so much attention now that Junior and Sissy are off on their own. Who would have realized that these friends were growing old before our eyes?

Many of us had been too busy making a living and raising the kids somewhere else to pay much attention to their presence in our lives. The Village Lifestyle seems to bring all of our realizations into focus as time passed; some of our old friends have left us. They are numbered among the memories that we hold closest. The void of their passing can only be filled by ... a new friend! That is what our friends are for! When friends pass, the void becomes painfully evident. A part of our connection with the past has left the present. But the void can quickly become a memory when we decide to risk our feelings and welcome a new friend. Amazingly, the pain reduces or vanishes when that bouncy little fur ball enters our lives. No time for painful reminiscing when there are all of these new, exciting experiences to share with our new friend.

Most of us have come here to create a new and better time and to make the most of our best years. New friends can help repair and rekindle old feelings from better times and better days and basically revitalize us. We relish those good, simple feelings, and the special kind of intimacy that these relationships can bring to a home. Nothing warms a space in our hearts and fills a home better than our friends. No matter what, they like us. Forgive us when we discipline them. And come back for more of the same, thank you! Who would have thought that toilet training (again) could be such a challenge and so much fun this time! Maybe we can see a lot of our selves, and our children, in them. Caring for someone else is good medicine. One thing is for sure. They will always be our friends.

Chapter Three

New Year's Resolutions from the Past

Resolutions and the Seasons in the Village

Getting Past Christmas: Some Suggestions.

The inevitability of death and taxes, and not necessarily in that order, and my experiences here with loss and grief in the passing of many Village Friends prompts me to offer to those of you who will experience this occurrence some suggestions:

a) Acceptance: No matter what you do, your Friend will probably precede you in passing. Remember that this fact is also fervently held by your children and family. You cannot turn back the hands of time on the clock.

b) Prepare: I would suggest that you come to a resolution with this fact, realizing that many years may pass before the final act.

c) Enjoy: Most of us here are on the downside of our years on earth in years. But there is a lot of living left out there, if you wish to make the most of it. Your Friend is blessed by God with a disregard for the portents of the future. That worrying has been left up to us humans. My profession has made such great strides in prolonging life in practically every category paralleling human medicine. My appraisal of the Village Friend Geriatric index is that the average canine Friend here lives to be 15+ (unless they eat too much!) and the average feline Friend lives to be 16+ (they worry less and lay around a lot!). Most geriatric illnesses that I have worked with in the Village circle around diet and exercise (sound familiar?). Most of the serious medical problems that I have encountered are treatable with modern veterinary techniques and medications. So the opposite of your worst fears exists in reality; you can prolong the life, in comfort, of your Friend for many years more now.

If A Loss Occurs: Most of us wish for a quick and painless passing to lessen the burdens on our loved ones. I wish for the same for your Friend. Whether that scenario occurs is not completely up to us. However, euthanasia is an option here, which I regard with the deepest respect and compassion. Prolonging suffering is not prominent any more in veterinary medicine simply because pain and suffering can be reduced with modern medicine. If that point comes when you cannot deal with your Friends infirmities any longer, not to worry. Your Friend does not have the capacity to hold grudges in this life or the next. In fact, they would give their lives for you in a heartbeat.

Internment: Due to the "rocky" nature of our Village soil, burying your Friend is not a good idea. Fortunately, cremation is a viable and affordable option here. The memories will remain with you and sustain you far longer than staring out a window at a gravesite. There is more reality and solidity in your memories than in the remains. Give your Friends a hug for me! Dr. Bob

1998-REMINISCENCES/1999-RESOLUTIONS

Fellow Villagers and Friends.

1998 was an eventful year for John Paul, Clifford, and me. We relocated from Corning, Arkansas, where Johnnie was born and raised. We left many friends and a few relatives. However, we quickly made many, many new friends, and have Grandma here more than in Corning! She really digs the Natatorium and the Thursday bridge sessions!

The opportunities here were so plentiful, and we took advantage of so many, that the results were very positive for our family. The Jessieville school system is a very fine educational and sports institution. I would say that the mixture of rural and Village children has done nothing but good things for everybody. The faculty and staff at Jessieville, and the facilities, are top notch. My veterinary experience here has been a dream come true. The feelings and regard that you have for your friends, lavishly applied in every case, have allowed me to practice quality and in depth medicine with many successes and cures for your friends. I must give you all a moment of silence for the friends that passed here in these lovely surroundings, among friends that cared for them and loved them very much. I have to tell you that everything that could be done to alleviate pain and suffering was done. I fully appreciate and agree with the very difficult decisions that some of you had to make. Wherever puppy and kitty heaven is located, besides in your hearts and memories, your friends are warm and comfortable, and fully fed everything they want, with no weight gain!

Some of you have moved forward and acquired new friends. I want to particularly thank those of you who adopted new friends from the Animal Shelter. Believe me; they greatly appreciate this "second life" and your attention and love. For those of you who have not selected new friends, or cannot believe that any kitty or puppy can ever replace your friends, give yourself time. You are correct in that no other pet can ever replace the memories. But life goes on. There are many friends waiting for a new home and a little personal attention. 1999 will be a good year for all of us Villagers and our friends. Clifford gets to come home next week so that he and Johnnie can have some of those adventurous walks that they are famous for. I for my part will continue to study, read, and improve my diagnostic skills so that I can cure, repair, and restore as many of your friends as I can.

Several projects are in the works regarding the wild critters of the Village. More will follow as these ideas take on form and function. I know that you will all have a very good 1999, friends and Villagers alike. So I thought that I would suggest some resolutions that will keep everybody healthy and happy: Villager Resolutions: I will cut down by half on treats per day to........ I will take more walks with ....I will get.....'S teeth checked and cleaned! I will find some method to keep those teeth clean. I will reduce the salt in ...'s diet. I will reduce the calories, especially fat, in ...'s diet. I will accept the fact that I and my friends now live in Arkansas in a subtropical climate. I will finally accept the fact that there are fleas and ticks in the Village and that some of them may find their way to my home and my friend from time to time.

Friend Resolutions: I will not chew, scratch, or destroy as much furniture, carpet, and draperies this year as I did last year. I will try harder to control my bathroom habits and will not use them to reproach my Villager(s). I will eat more of what is good for me. I will try to get along with my fellow Friends in the household a little bit better. I will agree to have a flea control product put on me once a month. I will take my medicine. I will give even more attention and love to my Villager(s) than ever before. I will renew my efforts to catch a ground squirrel or tree squirrel (even though I don't really know what I would do with one if I did catch it!). I will not dig in the flower beds for imaginary underground critters. I will bark less at passerby and not jump on visitors to my house.

NEW YEARS RESOLUTIONS (from your Friends!!)

We Villagers are all diligently preparing our New Year's Resolutions. So I thought I would give you a few requests from on behalf of your Friends based upon my personal experiences over the last Year. Looking forward to this year in service to the Friends in the Village in 2000!!

Resolved; that my Villager parents will not leave food down for me all the time. They don't do this for themselves!

Resolved; that I will use only the litter pan in the

utility room.

Resolved; that I will not make my parents throw out good food, simply because I am not hungry at the moment.

Resolved; that I will quit jumping up and down on everybody that comes to our home.

Otherwise, please call Mike Lewis so that he can teach me (and you) to prevent this bad habit.

Resolved; that my Villager parents will get me vaccinated for everything, since everything type of virus and disease is present in the Village.

Resolved; that my Villager parents will put Frontline on me very month or so, even if they don't see the fleas and ticks that bite me.

Resolved; that neither of my Villager parents will slip me processed foods as treats, which cause me to throw up and have diarrhea.

Resolved; that my Villager parents will realize that I am growing old and need an upgrade of the types of food that I eat, regardless of my resistance to change. They know what is best for me.

Resolved; that my Villager parents will bring me to Dr. Bob once a year for routine tests so that I will be treated for problems early in their course instead of waiting for disaster to strike.

Resolved; that all of my love and attention will be in the form of hugs and pats, and not burger patties.

Chapter 4

Your Friend's Body

The Body And Some Basic Functions

THE HEAD

Your Friends have all of the systems in their head that you possess. However, there is no hatred in there and very little envy!! The brain of your Friend is similar to ours with less of the portion for intelligence but closer to us in the memory area. The major nerves are all the same. Of course, the sense of smell (olfaction) and sight and hearing are far more developed. In fact, a doggy with a good nose can smell up to ten thousand times more accurately than we can.

The number of teeth in dogs and cats differs somewhat. The major teeth in the dog are the canines in front and the carnassial and big molars toward the rear. In cats the canines are the most important. Dogs and cats do not chew much, more like rip and tear and swallow.

THE MOUTH: Where It All Begins

You could say that the mouth is where everything begins for your friend. So this series of articles will deal with some of the most common problems of the mouth. Teeth, Tongue, Tonsils, and the lining of the mouth including the glands that supply various ingredients needed for chewing or removing certain harmful ingredients from the mouth will be discussed. Proper treatment of food while in the mouth is that important first step in the total health of your friend.

TEETH.

Both kitties and puppies have a set of baby teeth called temporary or deciduous that fall out over about a six month period. You have all undoubtedly found a few of these in your lifetime of having pets. Sometimes these temporary teeth do not fall out and must be removed by the veterinarian. The temporary canine or fang teeth are the most common ones to overstay their visit. If they stay they can cause decay. During evolution and breed development, the teeth have not changed much in size. So those of you blessed with the shorter faced friends may see teeth that have rotated or crowded in to a very short or small mouth. These crowded or jammed teeth provide places for food to lodge and decay to begin. Much can be done when your friends are young to reduce these problems. However, in your older friends, removal is usually the best solution.

Veterinary dentistry has come a long way in the past twenty years. Almost any dental problem can be corrected or relieved. In fact, I would say that the second most common medical problem that I observe in older friends is teeth problems. Bad teeth can affect everything from personality to liver function. Your friend's teeth hurt just as much as your teeth bother you. However, your friends don't complain as much as your aunt Minnie who has the partials and grinds them and complains about them. I have noticed an improvement in attitude in many patients who have had that bad tooth or all of that calculus removed from their mouth. Calculus is that hard buildup on the teeth. This product has to be removed by a dental pick or machine. You cannot brush calculus away once it builds up.

Dental review: Dogs normally have 28 temporary\42 permanent teeth. They can have more but often have less. The most important teeth are the canines (fangs up front) and the upper large maxillary (cheek) teeth which are used for chewing and tearing. The rest of the teeth between, in front or back of these primary teeth are not as necessary since our friends eat prepared food.

Our feline friends (cats) normally have 26 temporary/30 permanent teeth. Cats very rarely have more teeth but often have less as the molars in the back of the mouth are often missing. The canines (fangs) and cheek teeth in cats are most necessary for chewing. Because our friends eat mostly prepared food, they really don't get much chewing exercise necessary to maintain the strength of the bond of the teeth to the jaws. So teeth become loose and fall out a lot as our friends grow older. Let's face it. Neither our feline or canine friends pull deer down for dinner anymore. Although our feline friends do present us with an occasional furry prize gleaned from the yard or utility room! So now I must repeat those words we all shudder to hear; brush your friend's teeth, once they are cleaned by the vet! So you won't have to come back again for a long, long time. Don't use human tooth paste. It is not meant to be swallowed nor does it contain much abrasive because we humans have been conditioned to brush every day. Pet toothpaste comes in flavors and has lots of abrasive because we know in our hearts that you cannot brush your friend's teeth every day. Once or twice a week will be plenty. If you don't I can guarantee you that your friends will have tooth problems and experience unnecessary pain. So reserve a special treat that is only given after the twice weekly brushing. This should help. All of the other solutions to clean teeth in pets such as chew bones,

Chew sticks, rawhide, etc., are a long second best effort I am not saying your friend will ever appreciate dental care. But you are doing the right thing for them.

Realize fellow Villagers that your friends nutritional needs drive a billion dollar industry that enables you to cater to their every desire. (I did not say need!). The vast majority of pet foods and snacks on the market are adequate for the healthy, active, crossbred kitty or puppy dog. Crossbred friends are simply closer to the mix of their ancestors and are naturally selected, sometimes against your wishes! So these crossbred kitties and puppies, which I refer to as Arkansas everything (you can substitute your home state if they were acquired elsewhere!), can eat just about any pet food on the market and do just fine. However, we humans decided many centuries ago that we wanted certain traits of color, size, shape, personality, the list goes on. Our wishes have run rampant over the original ancestral origins of our friends. That is why there are now specialty diets and prescription diets for our purebred or mostly purebred friends. That is why there also are veterinarians who specialize in treating these friends of ours. Who devote their careers to figuring out what combination of food will work best for our friends.

THE EYE

Your kitty and doggy Friends possess a remarkable stereoscopic vision. They inherited this ability from their hunting ancestors. Both species can see some color. Your doggy Friend has an eye very similar to our eye with one focal point on the back of the eye. However, the kitty Friends is endowed with very good night vision. Their eyes are so sensitive to light that the iris can close to a slit in strong light resulting in two focal points at the top and the bottom of the closed iris. You have probably noticed this when your kitty Friend sits in the sunlight.

The eye consists of the following main structures; cornea, iris, lens, and globe or eyeball.

CORNEA, or clear portion of the eye that you can see, is the clear top of a container that holds the clear liquid, the aqueous humor in the front chamber of the eye. The cornea consists of layers like an onion. There are normally no blood vessels running through the cornea. Increased pressure in the eye can cause the cornea to cloud by squeezing the layers together. Disease can easily attack the cornea from the outside or inside of the eye. Thorns, cat claws, doors, and cars are the most common sources of trauma to the eye in my experience. The tears that cover the cornea are a constant source of protection. If there are not enough tears, the cornea will begin to dry out. This is very serious. A cornea that has been injured or irritated for several days will begin to develop little red blood vessels coming in from the edge. This condition must receive immediate treatment. Scrapes or pits in the cornea are called corneal ulcers. These are tears in one or more layers of the cornea. Repair is very slow. These injuries must be medicated until they completely heal. Sometimes the healing is not complete and a scar will result. The scar is usually white. This is simply an area where there is no living corneal tissue. Your friend can see around scars if they are not very large. If all of the layers of the cornea are penetrated down to the last layer, called Descemet's Membrane, your friend is in immediate danger of having the eye collapse. Fortunately, your veterinarian can perform a surgery to close the eyelids over the cornea and allow it to repair.

IRIS

The iris (uvea) is a circular bundle of strands of muscles, the center of which is that tiny whole (aperture), through which the light image is projected to the retina through the lens. These muscles can be damaged, become infected or inflamed (uveitis) and swell, bleed or stick to the lens (iris bombe). Much of the pain in the eye is located in these muscles. Iris color is hereditary. If the iris sticks to the lens (iris bombe), your veterinary ophthalmologist can unstick it. The iris is a very delicate system. Fear can cause a dilation of the iris. Certain medicines can also dilate or constrict the iris. This is known as the ciliary body. It is a ring of muscles in various colors that open and close to let in light through the center of this ring.

LENS

The lens is suspended behind the iris (that colored part of your friend's eye). There are little elastic fibers that hold the lens in perfect alignment so that images that come through the small opening in the iris will be clearly projected to the retina. Your friends have lenses very similar in shape and structure to our human eye lenses. Trauma can cause one or more of these ligaments to come loose, causing the lens to drop or tilt. This could change the image on the back of the eye. The lens becomes cloudy as your friends age. This is called nuclear sclerosis and causes a small loss of vision. Kind of like the steam on your windshield. The lens can also develop a cataract. This is a bright white spot. There are many types of cataracts that can develop for many reasons. Many breeds of dogs have a high incidence of cataracts. Diabetic friends can develop cataracts also. Fortunately, veterinary ophthalmologists can remove cataractous lenses as routinely as our human counterparts.

CILIARY BODY: The tissue in the corner formed by the iris with the front chamber of the eye (anterior chamber) is where the clear liquid in the eye is produced. This area is called the ciliary body. This system of cells continuously produces a very clear liquid that flows into the front chamber of the eye. There is also a drainage point at this place in the eye where the liquid leaves the chamber. There is a pressure control system in place to prevent an abnormal increase or decrease in the pressure in this chamber caused by the presence of this fluid. If the pressure is too low, the front chamber will deflate like a balloon. This condition usually occurs from trauma.

GLAUCOMA: Increased pressure in the eye is much more damaging and can lead to blindness. The increased pressure can come from either too much fluid or a plugged drainage system. When the iris swells from inflammation or infection, the normal angle at which it attaches to the eye will partially or completely close the drainage system causing a pressure increase (glaucoma). An inflammation of the cells that secrete the fluid can cause an overload of fluid also causing an increase in pressure. The aging process can cause a sagging of the iris and the eye with a partial closure of this drainage system. This type of angle closure glaucoma is quite common in dogs as they age but rarely occurs in cats. Glaucoma can be treated with some success. Currently, veterinary ophthalmologists can partially freeze the tissues that produce the aqueous humor, that clear liquid in the front of the eye, and reduce the pressure significantly.

Eyelids and Eyes: Some Commonly Inherited Conditions

Since I have examined and treated several eyelid and eye conditions recently that can be connected with allergies, I thought I would review with you some of the most common conditions of the eyelids (palpebrae) and eyes and then deal with the most common conditions resulting from allergies on the Village.

Hereditary Conditions of the Eyes and Eyelids

Entropion: Doggy friends can be born with a turning in of the eyelids. This causes irritation to the cornea by the lashes brushing against it. This rolling in of the eyelids is surgically correctable.

Ectropion: Our doggy friends may also have loose-fitting eyelids. These can cause a pooling of tears or create a pocket for dust and foreign particles to collect. This condition is surgically correctable.

Trichiasis: This condition is an irritation of one or both eyes by the projection on to the eyeball of extra eyelashes or hair. The patch of hair can be removed by surgery.

Distichiasis: This condition occurs when eyelashes protrude from an abnormal follicle from an unusual location on or under the eyelid. Surgical removal will correct this.

Corneal scratches: These injuries are the most common irritation to one or both eyes. The scratches are visible with an ophthalmic stain. They usually resolve in three days with vigorous treatment.

Corneal ulcers: These are deep erosions in one or both eyes. They can be the result of an injury or simply be created by improperly fitting eyelids.

Dermatitis pigmentosa: This condition is a black pigment that spreads very slowly over the cornea. The condition is usually in both eyes. This pigment comes from a continued low-level irritation to the corneas. Common in Peke, Lhasa, and Shih-tzu breeds or crosses where a facial fold pushes hair into the eyes. This can be treated with surgery in some cases, and just medication in others.

Allergy symptoms in our Friends closely parallel our allergy symptoms.

Allergic blepharitis: this condition is quite common in the Village. The eyelids become irritated with no corneal ulcers. There usually is a lot of tear flow in this condition. Your Friend may also rub the eyelids because they itch. The itching can also be a contact dermatitis caused by medication, pollens, and cigarette ashes, anything foreign to the body (allergens). When the eyelids are rubbed very hard by your friend, they can swell immediately.

Treatment: Flush the eyes with liquid tear (methyl cellulose) in case there is a foreign substance in the eye. Water will also work. Visine is ok... You should keep some solution on hand for such occasions. If the irritation continues, seek veterinary help.

Conjunctivitis: This is a reddening of the whites of the eye. If there is no foreign substance present in the eyes after flushing with the liquid tears, then consider allergic conjunctivitis. I have found a lot of this condition in the Village.

Third eyelid disease (cherry eye, "Hawes"). These colorful names will give you some idea of how common this condition is in our country doggy Friends. When the third eyelid, which both cats and dogs have, becomes irritated, a gland inside the eyelid can become permanently swollen. I have never seen this condition in a cat. Most of these glands do not reduce in size. Surgical removal of this gland will correct the problem.

The "Food Tube": Mouth-Esophagus-Stomach-Intestines-Colon

AN UPDATE; Chewing, Digesting, And Eliminating - The Big Three!

One of the daily pleasures that we Villagers and our Friends enjoy is eating. Nothing is more satisfying to us than to see a hearty appetite in our Friends as they eagerly gobble up what we have prepared for them. In fact, this simple but necessary daily routine is one of our primary ways to show them that we care about them. Most of us spend a substantial amount of our day planning and preparing that tasty offering to our Friends in the hope that our efforts will be rewarded with a wagging tail or a satisfying purr.

We are providing our Friends with the necessary nutrients for life. They depend upon us for this vital service. Otherwise they MAY raid the trash, go outside and catch a mouse or lizard, look for garbage, or simply go next door and get our neighbors to feed them! For simplicity's sake I will review the major differences between our digestive systems and our friends so that you can understand what happens when your friend eats that tasty meal.

The digestive systems of our dog friends are quite similar to ours. So they "enjoy" most of the same good and bad results from eating the right foods and snacks and suffer equally from eating the wrong things. Our doggy friends have the digestive system of a six month old baby and generally stay at that level for most of their lives. So consider what you fed your kids at 6 months of age as a way to decide what to feed them.

Kitty cats are not quite like us. They do not synthesize any vitamins in their systems. They are still designed to be occasional eaters although you wouldn't think that from the way some of them eat. They are designed beautifully to fast. Not so good to eat all of the time. Kitty cats are still very close to their hunting ancestors in their habits, which are no surprise to those of you who enjoy their company and try very hard to please their picky appetites. Because they are wonderful "fasters", they can wait until you present what they really, really want. Both cats and dogs do not have the same enzymes in their mouths that we do. So their chewing of food doesn't do much. That is probably why they gulp their food, eh? Once the chewed food reaches the stomach it is churned and acidified. This stomach acid starts to break down the chewed food. Then this "slurry" is emptied a little at a time into the small intestine where an organ called the pancreas adds products that neutralize the acid and continue to break down the proteins, fats and carbohydrates in the food. The liver provides bile at this point. The food in this neutral, pre-digested form now proceeds through the many loops of the intestines where the nutrients are absorbed into the blood stream through the walls of the intestines. What is left arrives at the colon where water is absorbed, bile is turned brown, and wallah! You have a stool to view shortly. This is bliss, fellow Villagers. An uneventful meal and a normal, formed brown (or some variation of brown) stool, or "bm" as we Midwesterners politely call the product. Any deviation from brown and formed may be a problem.

THE CHEST (THORAX) The "Heart" Of The Body!

This portion of your friends' body contains some vital organs, protects the spinal chord, and provides support for movement. The structures are similar for both our feline and canine friends.

VERTEBRAE & RIBS: The chest (thorax) generally contains twelve vertebrae and Twenty-six ribs, counting both sides. At the entry to the chest, the collar bone on dogs is rigid and fixed, while the cat collar bone "floats" and is not attached at one end. Helps Explain why they can jump so effortlessly on to the kitchen counter where you left the Shrimp! The chest is also connected and reinforced by a breastbone (sternum) that attaches the first seven ribs while the last six generally "float" by one attachment to the Spinal column with only a cartilage connection to the sternum. The back bone is very rigid with very strong ligaments and muscles. It does not flex very much. The ribs are Connected along the backbone. Injury to this area is usually to the ribs as they are the weakest part. If more than two ribs in a row are broken, it would be difficult for your friend to breathe. This is called a "flail chest" and usually occurs from severe injuries.

ORGANS INSIDE THE CHEST: The vital organs of the chest are; spinal chord, heart, lungs, blood vessels and nerves, esophagus, diaphragm. If you could look inside your Friends chest from the left side you would see only a small wedge of the heart as the lungs are wrapped around the heart. This space on the left side of the chest is where the Veterinarian listens best for heart sounds. The windpipe, esophagus, and blood vessels inside the chest are surrounded by the left and right lungs in a space called the mediastinum (or "middle space"). This space is often the first place for fluid to accumulate in the chest in early heart disease, pneumonia or from trauma. A severe blow to the chest can cause the heart to "bounce" against the inside of the chest bones resulting in bruised heart muscles or accumulation of blood inside the sac (pericardium) that covers the heart, which can be life-threatening (cardiac tympanode). The backside of the chest cavity is closed in by the diaphragm, a thin sheet of muscles that is vital to breathing.

SPINAL CORD: The vertebrae over the chest contain a canal which protects the spinal cord as it continues down the body. Damage to the spinal cord in this region of the body is rare. Occasionally a disc ruptures here, causing bruising of the chord.

HEART: The heart in both cat and dog Friends pumps the used blood into the lungs and pumps the freshly oxygenated blood out into the body. The dog and cat heart contains four chambers and is very similar to the human heart in all functions and has the same possibilities for disease as the human heart. There are four chambers, right and left ventricle (these do the most work), right and left auricle (very thin-walled chambers). The main blood vessel to the lungs carrying the low oxygen (blue) blood is the pulmonary artery. This comes from the right ventricle. The main blood vessel to the body is the aorta. It comes from the left ventricle. Heart size in your friends can be as different as Their breeds , sizes, and body shapes.

LUNGS: Your friend has two lungs with several Parts called lobes. These organs are basically bags of little air sacs called alveoli, that exchange oxygen (inhale) for carbon dioxide (exhale) across a very thin membrane. The low oxygen blood circulates around these sacs and transfers carbon dioxide out. Through a transfer process oxygen is captured and transforms the old blood into new, bright red oxygenated blood. The lungs get air from the windpipe along two main delivery tubes (bronchi), that continue to divide down to very small bronchioles that connect to those alveoli I mentioned previously.

BLOOD VESSELS AND NERVES IN THE CHEST

The major blood vessels in the chest are the pulmonary artery and aorta, which I have mentioned previously, and the coronary arteries. The coronary arteries supply blood to the heart muscle. They are the first vessels leaving the aorta with the freshest blood supply so the heart will continue to beat. The coronary arteries rarely plug up as is the norm in our senior citizens. The pulmonary artery is really a vein because it carries used blood back to the lungs. The pressure needed to move this used blood into the lungs is low compared to the pressure in the aorta, or main artery from the heart to the body. The aorta carries freshly oxygenated blood to all parts of the body. The pressure here is very high as there is a lot of territory to supply and a lot of resistance from muscles. Your friends rarely have hardening of the arteries. They do not have cholesterol problems as we do. Aneurisms, or weakened blood vessels, are rare. Most problems with the blood vessels in the chest come from trauma.

Esophagus

This organ continues its direction from the mouth to the stomach through the chest cavity. It passes into the front of the chest along with the windpipe and major blood vessels, arteries, and nerves. It passes over the top of the heart and goes through the diaphragm to enter the stomach. If there is a blockage in the esophagus, it generally is over the heart where the esophagus passes between the windpipe stems and the major blood vessels of the heart. Some dilations or constrictions of the esophagus can be inherited also. However, they usually show up at weaning when solid food is taken. Damage from blockage can result in a permanently stretched area called megaesophagus. This condition can cause pooling of food or liquids in the esophagus. Very difficult to treat or repair because of the location but very rare.

Diaphragm

This organ is a thin curtain of muscles that close off the back of the chest from the lumbar and abdominal regions of the body. These muscles contract and expand to pump air into and out of the lungs. All of the blood vessels to the rest of the body and the esophagus pass through this organ. There is a fragile seal around everything that passes through these muscles to the rest of the body. The seal around the esophagus can be damaged, causing a hiatal hernia.

Some of your friends are born with this condition. Cats jumping from great heights can dislodge the esophagus at this point and cause a hernia. Occasional vomition can be a sign of a hiatal hernia, but it is rare. In severe cases, the intestines can come through the Opening into the chest cavity and affect breathing.

Next week, the abdomen (belly) and lower back. Please give your Friends a hug for me!! Dr. Bob

"Heart to Heart"

Fellow Villagers, it is time for a serious talk about a serious problem that will probably visit your friends as they age, if not already. The good news in this serious talk is that modern veterinary medicine and the latest human medications are available for your friend, should a heart condition develop. The bad news is that this is the most overlooked condition in diagnosing your friends. I am instituting a "Senior Wellness Plan". that will include a complete physical, EKG, ultrasound, complete laboratory tests including urinalysis. Why? Because early diagnosis of heart disease in your dear friend is as important as it would be to you. Secondly, because I can maintain and reduce the onset of heart conditions and the symptoms that will occur, for a substantially longer period of time compared to doing nothing until the severe symptoms appear. The severe symptoms are ; coughing, exercise intolerance, discolored gums, labored breathing (dyspnea). There are many "overlapping" symptoms that can also confuse this. There are three basic categories of heart disease; a distended heart muscle/chamber, a bad valve (mitral/tricuspid insufficiency) and a thickened heart muscle. The more infrequent conditions like fluid in the heart sac (pericardial tympanode), atrial fibrillation, holes in the wall of the heart (septal defect), or atherosclerosis (plugged coronary arteries) account for a very small percentage of heart conditions.

Most of these heart conditions first develop with a small accumulation of fluid in the area around the heart outside of the heart sac (pericardium). This "hilar fluid" usually causes a cough or a slightly noticeable difficulty with exercise.

Modern Medications: The general drugs most frequently used for heart disease in veterinary medicine are; Enacard (which is human Vasotec). This drug helps the circulation and gives some relief to the kidneys, and lowers blood pressure. Lasix. This is a diuretic used by humans and friends and causes urinating so that the fluid will not collect in the chest around the heart. Digitalis; veterinarians generally use Digoxin, a form of digitalis, because it is safer. This drug causes the heart muscle to beat stronger and at a more steady rate. There are many other cardiac medications for specific conditions. However, these are the basic medications used.

The Failing Heart: What to Look for!!

I have examined and am treating many of our canine and feline friends that have heart failure in various stages. I wanted to give you some simple signs to look for. These are all common sense. Heart disease is not a new matter in the Village. Many Villagers are dealing with this matter of their own heart health on a daily basis. The same situation can exist for your Friend. So these are my primary signs for the beginning of a failing or malfunctioning heart.

1) Exercise Intolerance. This is usually the first sign of a laboring heart. Your doggy friend has

probably been going on very long walks with you as you recapture that magnificent stamina that you possessed prior to beginning your exhaustive career that made you financially secure enough to move here. Remember that one of your big people steps is about 3-6 of your doggy Friends steps. Walking one human mile is many doggy miles! So your Friend, now that he or she has all of your time and attention, loves these walks. However, one day your Friend simply sits down and doesn't want to go any further. This is probably not obstinacy. Could be that proverbial running out of gas that we all experience from time to time. Or it could be heart disease.

2) Morning cough. When your friend first awakes in the morning, the first few steps are accompanied by a soft cough. Could be a nighttime accumulation of mediastinal fluid. A heart system that begins to fail has a fluctuating blood pressure . The kidneys secrete hormones that constrict the blood vessel system of the body, causing hypertension. This up and down pressure change in the body can result in fluid "backing up" from the system and accumulating in the space around or between the lungs. This fluid presses on the windpipe at a cough center located where the trachea divides into two sections, causing a cough. As the heart loses efficiency, the cough can increase in frequency or severity. Of course, there are other reasons for a cough including bronchitis. But a persistent, soft cough can be an early sign of a failing heart.

3) Fluid accumulation in the abdomen. This condition, called ascites, is an excessive accumulation of fluid in the abdomen. This fluid is outside of the blood system; is generally clear, and can add pounds to

your friend in a relatively short time. Now I am not talking about the acceptable "pillow", or "love handles" that are well-earned rewards of the good life here in the Village! This condition is called a "pendulous abdomen". Kind of looks like pregnancy, (I am told). One or more of these early warning signs will indicate to your veterinarian whether it is time for an EKG, laboratory tests, and a chest x-ray or ultrasound. I have diagnosed several early heart conditions in our aging Friend population. Due to the modern advances in human medicine, our Friends are now benefitting from many "human" heart medications. However, these medications can also be very dangerous. I have visited with some Friends that have been taking one or more of these medications without previously having a minimum of an EKG, complete blood work and chest x-ray. Ask yourself how many medical cardiologists would prescript to you any heart medication without doing these diagnostic workups to see which condition that you have. Ask yourself how many of them would not insist on checkups and routine tests to make sure the medication is still effective and the dosage is still appropriate. Ask yourself why you would not insist on the same for your Friend!! Please give your Friends a hug for me!! Dr. Bob

THE ABDOMEN; Other Organs

This region of the body contains the rest of the vital organs of the body. Each organ Will also be discussed in later articles on a more detailed basis because all of their functions cannot be covered in one article.

The abdomen of your friend's body begins at the diaphragm and extends back to the rectum or rear of your friend. Vital organs are necessary for life. In modern veterinary medicine there are many medications which can be used as supplements to sustain life when an organ is failing. However, it is still impossible to completely replace all substances produced by organs for any length of time. The organs of the abdomen are: stomach, liver and gall bladder, pancreas, Intestines, kidneys, adrenals, spleen, ovaries or testicles, and bladder.

Stomach: This organ is a dilation of the tube from the mouth to the rectum. It contains a specialized lining that secretes hydrochloric acid and mucous. There are several thin layers of muscles on the outside of the stomach that expand and contract in a "washing machine" effect to break up the bulky food that enters the stomach.

Liver: This organ performs many functions needed by the body for life. Your friend's liver has about six times the necessary tissue to function. A lot of damage can occur before normal function is reduced. All of the blood that flows through the liver passes through a system of tubes where products are delivered into the blood stream. There are over six-hundred different functions and interrelated functions performed by liver tissue.

Gall bladder: This little bag is tucked away in a pocket in one of the four lobes of the liver. "Gall" or bile is a liquid secreted by this little balloon-shaped organ that spills into the upper intestine, aiding in the breakdown of fats. Your friend can live without a gall bladder, as do many humans.

Pancreas: This vital organ produces enzymes to digest fats, proteins, and carbohydrates. Also produces bicarbonate to neutralize the acidic material from the stomach and insulin to permit active absorption of sugar (glucose) from the blood into the cells of the body.

Kidneys: Your friends all generally have two kidneys. These organs filter the waste from the blood (urea), and form the liquid we all know as urine. Water and salts, primarily sodium, are retained or discharged by the kidneys to maintain the vital sodium, potassium, chloride balance in the body. Any major excess or deficit of any or all of these electrolytes, as we call them, can be fatal. The kidneys have about two Or three times the functional tissue necessary to maintain a healthy system. If the kidneys do not remove urea from the blood; the excess will cause "uremia" or uremic poisoning as we know it. This is fatal if not removed from the blood because urea poisons the cells in the body.

Adrenals: These very small organs or located on top of each kidney. Your friend will die in a matter of hours without these organs. They produce the natural Steroids in the body necessary for life. Many of the steroids or hormones that are dispensed by your veterinarian for disease, allergies, deficiencies of many sorts, are synthetic or look-alike compounds for the corticoids produced by the adrenals. Spleen: This organ stores blood cells, filters the blood, produces many immune cells for the body. Your friend can live without this organ, but will be highly prone to infection and disease. This organ swells in response to stress, trauma, heart conditions, or disease.

Ovaries or Testicles: These are the trouble-making

organs of the body without which your pet can do very nicely! They are important for reproduction. The hormones produced by ovaries and testicles are responsible for all of the mating behavior for both your female and male Friends. Spaying (removing the ovaries) in your female Friends removes both the behavior and the Potential for pregnancy. The cat and dog uterus is Y shaped as compared to the human triangular shaped uterus. This Y is necessary to provide room for many (multiparous) puppies or kitties. I recommend early surgical removal of the uterus before your female Friend comes "into heat". There are far too many unwanted and unnecessary births among the dog and cat population of this world. No, they should not have a litter or a first "heat" cycle before they are spayed. The testicles in your male Friends produce sperm and testosterone, the former for reproduction, and the latter for the idea to reproduce. Testosterone in your male Friends has a half life of about eighteen days in the system for male behavior. Early neutering precludes most unacceptable male behavior. However, behavior can also become a habit. The most troubling habit is male "marking" in the house. Early neutering of male doggy Friends will generally prevent this unwelcome habit. I routinely neuter male cats and dogs at 4 ½ months. The surgery and recovery time is minimal and less traumatic to the patient and parents! Removing the reproductive organs of your Friends does not require hormone supplementation as in humans because the male and female hormones in your friends are produced in small quantities in other tissues in their bodies. In later life, however, some small group of female friends can begin to lose control of the muscles that control voluntary urination. So they may require hormone therapy to regain some of that control and prevent the "bed-wetting" that sometimes occurs.

Bladder: This organ collects urine from both kidneys through (ureters) and then delivers the urine to the outside, hopefully not your carpet!), through the urethra. This organ is usually very thin but will thicken from any stress and become sore. Bladder inflammation is very common in our domesticated friends, possibly because they have to hold their urine so long in the house!

However, our friends share our stresses so they can be expected to develop this some time in their life. Our cat friends have this most often, with the male cat friends being the largest group.

The Urinary System

Both your feline and canine friends have a urinary system. This includes kidneys, ureters, bladder, and urethra. The kidneys, second to the liver and heart, are some of the most vital organs in the body. Without them, your friends would die in a matter of hours, unless they were on dialysis. The kidneys have four main functions:

1) Conservation of water and electrolytes in order to maintain a constant balance in the body water environment: The main electrolytes in the body are Sodium, Potassium, and Chloride. These are called electrolytes. They exist in a standard percentage or amount. If one or more of them increases or decreases significantly, your friends will develop serious symptoms, lose their balance, or even have seizures. If

the balance is not maintained, destruction will take place. Most electrolyte imbalances occur when your friends vomit, have diarrhea, or urinate too much or too little. These losses or gains in electrolytes generally occur rapidly, in a matter of hours or less. The kidneys cannot maintain a balance in the presence of such a rapid change. Basically, the kidneys retain or release excess electrolytes to maintain the balance. Since kidneys are supplied by the body's blood system, an electrolyte imbalance can also damage them, reducing their functional ability, while they are trying to do their job. Since the body is a giant internet (current term!), any damage or disruption in one part can affect the kidney. Infection, disease, poisoning, can all damage the kidneys and reduce function.

2) Elimination of waste products: the kidneys remove some of the waste products of digestion, mostly urea from the body in the urine. Urea is a waste product of the metabolism of protein. Too much or poor quality protein in your friends diet will cause the kidneys to work very hard. Over a long period of time this overwork can simply wear out the kidneys. If the kidneys do not remove the urea efficiently, this waste product can build up in the blood and damage the body. Uremia is an excessive amount of urea in the body and can be fatal. I would say that the primary cause of death in our older friends is uremia from kidney failure. So diet quality is everything.

3) Balancing and producing certain hormones; erythropoietin and renin are necessary for life functions of the body. The kidneys produce a hormone that stimulates the production of erythropoietin. The kidneys also produce renin. These products are necessary for stimulating the very basic functions of

cell production in the body. A deficiency in either of these hormones is eventually fatal. Erythropoietin is necessary to stimulate the production of the most basic cells in the body for many uses. Renin is produced by the kidneys to take part in a vital process called the renin-angiotensin II-aldosterone system for regulating the electrolyte balance of the body. This is the system whose dysfunction produces hypertension, or high blood pressure in your friends. Eventually hypertension leads to heart failure.

On the flip side of this, a reduced heart output of blood can reduce nutrition to the kidney tissue, reducing the ability of the kidneys to produce these products, resulting in an imbalance. So it is not always the kidneys that start these problems! Veterinary pathologists say that the tests of kidney function most commonly used are the BUN and Creatinine. The BUN is Blood Urea Nitrogen. This is an accurate test that measures the amount of urea still in the blood. A high amount means that the kidneys are not actively removing this waste product.

Creatinine is a waste protein created by body metabolism. Since the body does not use or reuse creatinine, it is excreted by the kidneys. It is our most reliable indicator of kidney function. In our friends, a creatinine value of more than one (1.0) indicates that processes are beginning to break down. Of course, dehydration can also increase this value. So a complete blood picture must be taken to understand why a value for creatinine is elevated. I have seen many of our feline or canine friends with high values for creatinine and/or bun that have survived for quite a while on a high quality protein diet. So common sense tells you to feed your older friends the very best. I have found that the 6-7 year age group is the time for this change to a higher quality diet. A geriatric blood test panel is also a necessity if you want to do all that you can for your friends' health. Please give your friends a hug for me! Dr. Bob

Your Friends Urinary System - What it is and How it Works

Your friends have the same basic urinary system that you have. They have two kidneys, a ureter that transfers the urine from each of the kidneys to the bladder. The urine is collected in the bladder and then is emptied through a urethra and out into the outside or the litter box....hopefully!

The normal method of production of urine is involuntary. Both your feline and canine friends produce about 1 milliliter per hour with normal water drinking. A milliliter is one sixth of a teaspoon. Urine is collected in the normal bladder until the pressure from the urine causes your friend to want to empty (void). Incontinence is the inability to control the emptying of the bladder. This can occur from inflammation, irritation, too much urine accumulation, loss of muscle control around the bladder, or loss of nerve control of the bladder system. This last condition can also result from loss of mental control, or senility. Kittens are generally more in control of their urination. As soon as they determine what a litter box is for, your problems are over. Of course, puppies are a different story. House training a puppy is difficult. Most puppies cannot hold their urine for more than a couple of hours. Puppies also will "mark" their territory or "den", which is your house. The natural instinct of a puppy is to urinate where some carnivore or predator will not discover their scent. So they may think it is safer to urinate in your house instead of in the yard! This is not true incontinence. Very few puppies or kittens ever have a urinary defect at birth. There are some reports of unusual conditions involving the bladder or urinary system. Most urinary problems in young to middle aged dogs and cats are due to infection, inflammation or situational trauma. Separation anxiety is one reason for inappropriate urination. However, this is not incontinence.

OLDER FRIENDS. Our aging population of senior friends will probably experience urinary incontinence at least once in their lives. Probably more. Older friends can develop cancer of the bladder or various other places in the urinary system. Diagnostic tests including testing tissue for cancer will determine the problem. Cancers of the bladder are diagnosed more frequently today because clients permit us to take samples for pathology. However, the most common reason for incontinence in a senior is an inflammation of the bladder. These inflammations are usually sterile at the first occurrence. That is why we treat without culturing the urine for bacteria on the first occurrence. Fortunately our pet food industry has given us wonderful support in the dietary department. Many bladder conditions can be controlled with a change to a medical diet. In any case, the symptoms and response to medication are much easier to control with diet. If you can persist in changing your friend's dietary preferences, you will be doing them a great favor. Remember that no friend will starve to death. That is hardly a problem in the Village!

URINALYSIS. This simple test is done in the clinic. The results are very accurate and give a lot of information. We can determine what part of the urinary tract is involved, some types of cancers, bacteria, nutritional, and medical conditions like diabetes. Once the type of urinary condition is diagnosed, some other matters are considered and a treatment prescribed.

MEDICAL DIETS: ASH IN THE FOOD. The low ash controversy in the pet food industry has come and gone. There is currently no reason to feed a low ash food over a high ash food. I just know that the medical diets clear up most or all of the urinary problems that I see. Even home cooking is not as good. The medical diets are generally low in ash. They also contain acidifiers and very high quality ingredients. The success rate of medical diets is very high. Once a friend has improved with a medical or special diet, returning to the old diet is not recommended. Special diets cost more, but reduce pain and suffering in your friend. Prevention by diet is always less expensive than medical treatment!

STEROIDS TO TREAT AN INFLAMED BLADDER. Since most bladder conditions are inflammatory, treating with an anti-inflammatory, that is, a steroid brings good results. The low doses of steroids that are given to treat bladder inflammations do not generally cause or increase the possibility of an infection. Reducing the inflammation also reduces the pain. This permits your friend to regain control or to simply stop emptying the bladder because it is too sore to hold the urine.

ANTIBIOTICS TO TREAT AN INFLAMED BLADDER. A recurring bladder problem is treated with antibiotics and/or steroids depending upon the amount of pain and inflammation. The ph of the urine will indicate the type of antibiotic to use. A resistant bladder condition will require a urine culture to determine the exact bacteria, fungus, or organism that is causing the condition.

SURGERY. There are times when all medical efforts fail, or too much damage has been done to the bladder or the urethra. Our feline male friends can suffer permanent damage to the urethra and require an urethrostomy. This surgery removes the curve in the male cat's urinary tract. He can still urinate backwards into the litter pan. No back pressure! No pain or strain! Our canine male friends also occasionally must have the urethra redirected similar to a male cat. Probably a bit embarrassing but adds years of life! Our female feline and canine friends rarely have any difficulties with inflammatory situation.

BLADDER STONES. . Obviously, stones in the bladder will cause irritation, inflammation, and frequent urination that may or may not be blood-tinged.

STRESS. This last cause of urinary problems is very hard to determine. I personally believe that urinary problems that appear after a stressful situation in the household , a thunderstorm, or boarding, trips, etc., were simply conditions that were subclinical,(not evident yet) that were triggered into a clinical problem. Stress reduction for your friends is closely tied to your life style and your stress adjustments. The Village is a wonderful place to reduce stress in your life. When your friends sense that you are at peace with yourself, they will feel better also!

The Normal and Abnormal Stool (BM): Feces in the Dog and Cat

Your doggy Friends will have a formed brown stool in the frequency of the meals they consume. So frequent treats may throw "regularity" off somewhat. One or two a day is fine. Bile pigment stains the stool brown. However, bile begins as a yellow product, oxidizes to green, and then to brown in a timed sequence. So any of the other colors simply means the stool has not had time to be finished and has been prematurely eliminated. A white stool means no bile and a lot of undigested fat. This generally means a pancreatic problem. However, a large meal of bones can also produce a white stool, one time. A black stool contains oxidized blood, which can turn from red to black. That generally means that the blood comes from farther up the colon. A slimy stool means the colon is inflamed and is secreting a protective coating. A stool with green grass in it means your Friend has an upset, acidic stomach. A stool with fresh blood on it means the very terminal part of the colon is bleeding. Your Friends bleed much more easily than we do so blood in the stool is not as serious a matter but must be resolved as to its origin and cause.

Your kitty Friends rarely has anything but a formed stool. The same basic colors as the doggy stools apply. However, a severe pancreatitis or a pancreatic insufficiency rarely produces a white stool from excessive undigested fat in the stool. That is presuming your Friend has consumed a fatty meal... I have seen many bone eating Friends pass a white stool from the calcium in the bones. A hard stool is much more common in our less active kitty Friends, of which there are many in the Village.

Chapter 5

Some Common Medical Problems

Vomiting: "The Village Syndrome"

Since this is the most common ailment presented to me in the Village, I thought I would take you through some of the common sense methods which both I and you can use to decide where or why the vomiting is taking place. Your doggy Friends are by far the most noticeable and worrisome vomiters. Kitty Friends seem to regurgitate, upchuck, or vomit at will and whim. I have seen very little medical vomiting in all but the oldest Kitty Friends on the Village.

I hope that this explanation will assist you in dealing with this very common problem. First, a definition. Emesis is the medical term for vomiting. This action is a very complex action requiring many systems in the body for the resulting emptying reflex of the stomach. Your feline and canine friends can also vomit at will if they don't like something or are stressed. They don't have to be sick. Acute Vomiting; When your friend begins to vomit with no recent history of symptoms, the condition is termed acute.

The severity of the vomiting can also be classified into projectile or simple vomiting. Most of the time this vomiting, with no real warning signs, is caused by a food incompatibility or a foreign substance. Grass causes vomiting. However, it is generally consumed by your friend because of an upset stomach. Grass is not the reason. Something else started the upset. There is an unacceptable substance, or too much acid, in the stomach. Your friend wants to get rid of the stomach contents. Most of the grass-induced vomiting in the Village is due simply to food incompatibility and secondary hyper acidity, in my experience.

The second most frequent cause of acute emesis is from a viral or bacterial infection. In most cases, a virus will attack your friend's immune system, weaken it, and let bacteria invade the digestive system, resulting in vomiting. Your friend may be feverish. However, you cannot feel your friend's head nor can you tell by a dry or wet nose, whether a fever is present. Only a rectal temperature will indicate whether a fever is present. Infections and fever can cause vomiting and not be located in the digestive system.

Please remember that emesis is a protective mechanism of the body to simply attempt to rid the system of disease or the products of disease. Emesis from simple indigestion; Many of your friends simply have too much of the good life in the form of frequent snacks and excessive amounts of food. The occasional vomiting of undigested food and the urge to eat grass can be a sign. Simply eliminating all snacks for three days and reducing feeding frequency to twice daily should give you some idea if this is the problem. Since emesis is such a general reaction to many categories of disease, it can also be the first sign of a serious problem. Recurring emesis that does not respond to fasting in 24 hours may be a sign of a more serious condition. Dehydration; this condition is the first concern in vomiting. Fluid loss to the body can be very serious. Gator-Aide or Pedialyte are the common sources for fluid replenishment. However, you must give very small amounts to prevent more emesis. Solid food is not necessary in the first 24-48 hours. Sugared water; 1 tsp. per cup of water, is a simple way to keep up your friend's energy level while the condition is correcting itself. Next week; chronic (recurring) emesis. Give your friends a hug for me! Dr. Bob.

Chronic Vomiting or Regurgitation

Some of our Friends, because of age or severity of a previous disease, or because of inherited deficiencies in one or more of their systems, will become recurrent vomiters. I believe that "upchuck" is probably because a passive vomiting episode is more common. Regurgitation is simply upchucking undigested food very soon after consuming the food. This symptom usually indicates a passive cause. The most common causes are; eating too fast, eating something that is radically different in type or consistency from a normal diet (fried bacon, ham fat, pizza, pepperoni, a lizard), etc. These types of food or material generally come right back up. Poisonous substances are not always regurgitated or vomited. Grass is an emetic (vomiting aid) to our Friends. A bright green vomitus with grass in it is a sure sign of some form of indigestion. The mechanical problems involved in swallowing and digesting in the vomiting part of the digestive system are too complicated to list here. Your veterinarian will be able to differentiate those for you. I see a lot of indigestion in the Village Friends for very simple reasons.

HYPERACIDITY is by far the most common medical condition in our Friends in the Village. If your Friend has rather frequent bouts of upchucking, or you can hear gurgling or squeeging sounds in the intestines, or burps, or vigorous pursuit of any available grass or green things when outside walking, or an unwillingness to jump up on the bed or couch, then consider this as the most probable cause. A few doses of Pepto or a Tagamet can quickly and temporarily clear this up until the cause is found.

IRRITATED STOMACH OR PYLORUS. Many of our Friends here are borderline hyperacidics from a diet that does not completely agree with them but does not make them clinically ill. However, additional stress in their lives, good or unwelcome, can "put them over the top". Storms, too many treats, grand kids, parties, trips and neighborhood critters are the most common. However, I see many Friends that simply have grown old on a favorite food and treat routine that simply has begun to slowly disagree with their aging digestive system. I see this commonly at about 8-9 years of age. This is midlife for Villager Friends. Their digestive systems and efficiency are changing. Time for a change to a more senior or bland diet and find some new aging-friendly treats. This is also time for Tagamet, Zantac, or Pepsid. Many Village Friends are taking these antacids with excellent results.

The pylorus is that small muscular gate at the end of the stomach which lets the acidified stomach contents begin to leak into the upper intestine. I have found that many of our very senior kitty and doggy Friends can develop some problems with a pyloric sphincter that has been slightly or acutely irritated and has lost some function. This condition is very difficult to treat medically or surgically. Thinning the food is generally the only simple and effective way to manage this difficulty.

Constipation and Difficulty in Elimination

And Now the Other End! Two topics that are dear to my veterinary heart and occur quite frequently here among our Village Friends involve old kitty Friends who are irregular and old doggy Friends who go too much! Irregularity: This condition of the bowels in older cats occurs on a "regular" basis (pardon the pun). As our kitty friends gracefully age, their colon begins to stretch and distend. This condition is called megacolon. A dilated colon holds the stool as it is formed prior to elimination. Older cat Friends that develop this condition have difficulty in moving their bowels. Many do not have a BM each day. Many have difficulty and will develop some interesting pre-elimination habits, such as throwing themselves against a wall, running around a lot, meowing a lot, etc. If the stool is larger than your little finger, your Friend could be a candidate for megacolon.

Solution:

a) Buy a quality diet (not from the store), that will reduce the amount of waste in the food. (you are paying for that anyway).

b) Try small amounts of whole milk. (no, the

calcium will not bind them as much as the butterfat will move them).

c) Put them on a dietary supplement from the vet that can be given on a daily basis.

d) Add metamucil granules to their food. (A pinch a day....you know the rest!).

In extreme cases of irregularity in kitty Friends, where possibly the contraction ability of the colon is not good enough to eliminate, we can subscribe a medicine dear to the hearts of some Villagers called Propulsid (I did not make up this name!). However, this medication is very effective and should be adjusted in the clinic (instead of on your floor or carpet!).

Doggy diarrhea or malformed stools: Very common in the Village. Primary reason; eating all day. Remember that some of what goes in must come out. Three meals a day with snacks are not even good for you! As your doggy Friends age, they should receive one main meal per day, and a small snack. If you have a Friend who is having loose stools, the first thing to do is cut back on the frequency and volume of feeding. If this doesn't work, try the following:

a) Buy a prescription diet (not from the store)

b) Cook a bland diet for Poopsie.

c) Put Pink Bismuth on the food. If Poopsie won't eat it, he or she really isn't that hungry.

d) Break up a Pepto tablet into five or more pieces. (Six tablespoons of liquid Pepto in one tablet)

e) Cut out all of the snacks. (and make sure your husband stops feeding snacks also. This must be a coordinated effort).

Comments: Many of the treats on the market contain waste fiber that makes wonderfully large, soggy doggy stools. You pay for what you get in the doggy food business. Just because it drives Poopsie's taste buds wild doesn't mean that it is good for her/him. Cheese can slow the bowels down. Substitute a walk for a snack. (this goes for both of you).

Revelation: You all moved to Paradise to have health wealth and happiness. Your Friends would like to be healthy too. So apply the same discipline to their lives that you are trying to apply to yours. They don't shop and they don't cook! And give your Friends a hug for me!! Dr. Bob

That Cold, Wet Nose!!

Since everybody's mother passed this conundrum on to them about determining the health of a Friend by such an observation, I thought I would put some sense into this. Cold, wet nose: The nasal passage contains a mucous lining and some "turbinate" or swirly cartilages. When air comes in through the nostrils, it is swirled a bit so that it can be warmed before it is inhaled into the lungs. The tears produced in the eyes of your friends, cat or dog, are supposed to drain down little tear drains in the bottom nasal corner of the eyelid. These drains come down the side of the nasal passage inside the tissues and empty at the bottom of the nostril openings. If you look really close, and your Friend is particularly accommodating that day, you can see these little holes. When all works well, the nose is wetted with the tears from the eyes and all is cold and wet.

Warm, dry nose!! No fellow Villagers. Not necessarily sick: and here is why/ Dry eyes; not enough tears are shed. Some of our friends do not produce many tears. Bad drainage angle; many of our friends simply have an unfavorable angle so most of the tears run down their little faces. (Called epiphora; poodles, pekes, shih tzus, lhasas, and in betweens). Plugged tear duct. The tear duct can swell for many reasons and simply not allow tears to pass (dacryocystitis).

Plugged tear ducts: Full of debris; (can even be from immune difficulties. A Friend can have a very high fever and have a wet, cold nose. A friend can be relatively normal and have a warm, dry nose. So do not rely too heavily on this sign. Give your friends a hug for me!! Dr. Bob

The Flu- What To Do When the Flu Hits!!!

I have been diagnosing and treating a large volume of the flu here in the Village each January-March. Most of these cases cannot be attributed to food or treats. The symptoms start as simple vomiting and/or diarrhea which goes on for several days. All treatments have thankfully been successful. However, the common denominator has been more than six months since the Parvo booster. The patients are widely distributed around the Village. Probably sick coyotes or foxes.

Treatment: At the first sign of vomiting or stomach discomfort, withhold food. Sugared water, one tsp per Cup, Gatorade, Pedialyte, will do for hydration. Pepto Bismol or Pink Bismuth or tablets are just fine. If there is a problem at either end, these items will coat the GI tract for about two hours. Then you must repeat. Remember to wear pink or do this in a pink room!! The Pepto tablets are equivalent to six tbsp of the liquid. I strongly suggest Tagamet (cimetidine 200mg) ⅃ table three times daily for the first 24 hours. Whole tablets if you have a Friend over 20 lbs. Please remember that the Parvo vaccine does not cause a strong response from your Friend's immune system. That is why a mid-year booster is highly recommended. Be sure and have the Coronagiven with the Parvo as this vaccine increases the immune response from your Friend. You cannot isolate your Friend from the wildlife here in the Village. So vaccinate them please!! Give your Friend(s) a hug for me!! Dr. Bob

Is It the Flu?

I have recently seen a rash of vomiting and diarrhea incidents on the Village. Since the Flu is going through the Village and one would suspect that there is a connection; I thought that I would give you some facts so that you can determine what is going on with your Friends when they develop stomach problems and/or diarrhea. Young Friends get into everything. They eat sticks, crickets, lizards, and everything that you drop from the table (intentionally or otherwise). So you must rule out an improper item first. Give Pepto, or better yet, Pink Bismuth. This will coat the stomach and bring immediate relief until the item passes. If the vomiting continues for more than 24 hours, call me.

If your young Friend has not had a Parvo/Corona booster in the last six months, consider that also. The parvo/corona vaccines do not give a full year's immunity to every Friend. The virus is very small, resulting in a difficult and often insufficient response to a challenge by the virus. Your Friends carry Parvo and Corona virus continuously in the lining of the intestinal tract. Old Friends have generally stopped eating sticks, etc., or you have simply become more vigilant and swift! Most of the gastric problems I see in older Friends are due to a gradual loss of digestive efficiency. They have their favorite foods and will not change readily. Tagamet is a good remedy. Most of the digestive problems in our Senior Friends are due to acid reflux. Diarrhea is generally a reaction to too much acid in the food contents coming down the tract. The colon will simply eliminate the acidic stool contents. Pink Bismuth will help the current situation. However, if this is a repeat matter, the diarrhea will come back. Pepto and Pink Bismuth and other antacids generally work for about two hours and must be repeated. Tagamet works within thirty minutes and lasts 6-8hours. I haven't had any good results from Pepsi or Zantac excepting the most minor stomach problems in Friends. Give your Friends a hug for me!! Dr. Bob

Allergies ala Arkansas

Now that the first peek of fall has come and gone (that two days of below 50 degree weather), it is time for a primer for you new Villagers and a reminder for native Villagers concerning the ever-present allergens here in the Village. This semi-tropical wilderness that we all love so much does come with some trade-offs. Pollens and P.M.: There are pollens and other little secretions from the rich plant life produced here all year. The spring, summer, fall and winter pollens are simply produced for those particular natural reasons of that time of the year. The change of foliage that is just beginning will also produce a lot of fine particulate matter as the leaves dry and fall from the trees. The ground cover that is always in various degrees of decomposition and decay is also more exposed to wind and more readily blown into the air. If you and your Friends have been here more than one fall season, then you will react in typical allergy fashion to these now-familiar particles as you are now sensitized. Bugs: There are fewer bugs and other crawly critters out in these cooler months. Most of them have not left. They are simply resting up for spring! Many of them will try to enter your nice, warm houses for the winter. Periodic spraying with Permethrin or treatment by the pest control companies should handle this. Since there is little farming around here, we will not get the benefit of harvest-produced particulate matter.

Construction and the perpetual work on the existing and new golf courses will not stir much up. They are watered frequently. This current dry spell will waft a lot of matter into the air. However, some fall rain (instead of snow) will take care of that. Indoor heat: Any forced-air heating systems will have accumulated molds over the summer months from the alternating condensation effects of cooler air and the relatively high humidity of this tropical climate. As the heat kicks on, these molds will dry and then become airborne. Changing or cleaning filters once a week will help all of you. Those of you who are more industrious or desperate can have the ducts cleaned. If you have had your home for more than one winter, then these molds will generate the typical allergic response when they hit the nasal passages. Wheat: This grain, in its many forms in dog foods, contributes to itching. True food allergies result in bloody diarrhea in a matter of minutes. So food that does not contain wheat gluten does not make your friend itch. However, an allergy-prone doggy Friend will itch quicker if fed gluten since he/she is already "primed" with airborne particulate matter. Give your friends a hug for me! Dr. Bob

Seasonal Breathing Difficulties in the Village

Hold Your Breath!! Now that the winter season, or what passes for winter here in Paradise, is upon us, I thought I would pass on to you some observations concerning the breathing patters of your Friends. Kitty Friends: Any interference with breathing in or breathing out in your Kitty Friend indicates that there is trouble. 90% of the respiratory problems in Kitty Friends are obstructive. There is difficulty breathing in or out because something is interfering with the normal flow of air. Most of the time, this obstruction is fluid of some kind. The most common fluid is mucous. The fall flu season does not spare our Kitty Friends. They can develop an upper respiratory infection without going outside or being directly exposed to other Kitty Friends. Of course, if they are routinely vaccinated for the common upper respiratory viruses, they will have both direct and indirect immunity to most viruses. One of the weakest systems in our Kitty Friends is their respiratory system. Sneezing is not normal for them. Nor does sneezing always indicate allergies. Excessive grooming is the most common symptom of allergies. I have seen several Kitty Friends from isolated homes who do not go outside, that have developed severe upper respiratory problems. Fortunately, their Village Mom and Dads brought them to me promptly. The other 10% of breathing problems in Kitty Friends are due to heart and lung problems.

There is a Feline Asthma condition. Our Kitty Friends do not develop a true asthma or emphysema. However, the terms are most familiar to people so we use them. These Kitty Friends are usually at least six years old. They do not have fluid in their chests or runny noses. They just breathe hard. The small percentage of our Kitty Friends over 12 years of age develop heart conditions associated with hyperthyroidism. This enlarged heart does make it harder to breathe. However, this is usually not noticeable. An annual thyroid test and chest x-ray can identify this problem and correct it, in most cases. Exercise intolerance is not noticeable in our Village Felines!! Unless you move the food bowl a few feet further than normal. I expect that they will not eat until you return the bowl to the "proper place"!! . Give your friends a hug for me: Dr. Bob

Oxygen in the Body

Respiration depends in a large part upon the oxygen content of the blood. So an anemic Kitty (low amount of red blood cells), will breathe more rapidly to try and take in more oxygen. This Increased rate of breathing is usually noticed when our Friend is in the usual reclining position doing basically nothing. Diaphragmatic hernia: This condition, wherein the diaphragm is torn, results in the intestines gradually filling in to the thorax (chest) between the lungs, and preventing them from expanding fully. This condition is almost always associated with trauma (jumping off of the roof), or being hit by a car. Surgery is the only way to correct this one.

Asthma: There is an asthma-like condition in kitty Friends. However, it is not a true asthma. Steroids will usually cure this, once it is accurately diagnosed. Emphysema: This condition results in little tears or holes in the lungs. Very rare in kitty Friends. Allergic bronchitis: This is a common condition in those few Villager homes where smoking occurs. Generally only indoor/outdoor kitty Friends contract this condition. Pneumonitis: This condition is actually quite common and can occur spontaneously in the most protected Villager homes. I believe that this condition can be caused by many different viruses under many different circumstances. This generalized inflammation of the lung tissues is painful and generally accompanied by a fever. This condition can quickly progress into pneumonia, which is very dangerous in kitty Friends.

Pneumonia: This is fluid in the lungs, either inside or outside the air pockets (alveoli). This condition is usually fatal if not treated quickly. Often no treatment is completely successful.

Stertor (loud breathing): This condition is caused by resistance or blockage to the main wind pipe somewhere between the lungs and the mouth. Damage anywhere along the wind passage can result in this condition. The noise may be temporary or permanent depending upon the cause. The cure is also relative to the severity and location of the problem. My advice: Keep your kitty Friends vaccinated and isolated from other kitty Friends (raccoons, bobcats, and foxes included!). There is no point in having "visits" from other kitty Friends. The risk is not worth it! Give your Friends a hug for me! Dr. Bob

Adverse Food Reactions: A Primer On What to Look for in Food

There are many adverse reactions to food that your friends eat that are minor. However, I thought I would give you the latest in terminology and the latest thoughts from the veterinary profession on this matter. Realize that reactions are seldom life threatening. Your friends are very good at "upchucking" or vomiting, as we can all verify. There are many other medical reasons for vomiting, so consider food incompatibility first.

The following terms are used by the American Academy of Allergy and Immunology.

FOOD ALLERGY: An adverse reaction to a food or food additive with an immunologic basis. This reaction would not necessarily show up in an external symptom. Laboratory tests would show a high lymphocyte percentage. Friends with this problem would not necessarily throw up or have diarrhea. However, those I have diagnosed just don't feel well. They lie around and seem to be in mild pain. There are many medical conditions in our Friends that can have this symptom, called "general malaise". Ah, those French have a way with words!! Removing different foods or additives from the diet "by elimination" is the standard method for curing this. I find that wheat gluten is the number one cause of food allergy. It is in many foods and treats. I have not decided yet if corn gluten is a problem or not.

FOOD INTOLERANCE: A nonimmunologic, abnormal physiologic response to a food or food additive. This is the old familiar diarrhea and vomiting problem that we see. The food does not have to be spoiled or a bad food. A sudden change to bacon or chili or anything different from a standard, stable diet can cause this. The usual response is a quick vomiting episode. Once the food is out of the stomach, all goes back to normal. The matter goes away when you stop that particular treat!

FOOD ANAPHYLAXIS: An acute systemic reaction to a food or food additive with respiratory distress, collapse of the blood vascular system, and itching. This condition is very rare as all pet foods are extensively tested for any difficulties such as this. I have seen this in Friends that eat lizards, frogs, insects, etc... The response is severe. They itch a lot and generally have hives all over or swell up in the face and neck area. This is a medical emergency requiring fast action on your part and a vet visit.

DIETARY INDISCRETION: This term, which we all have violated at one time or another refers to overeating, eating unusual things such as dirt, and eating grass or one's own stool (bm). The simple cause of this is food not being completely digested before it passes as stool. Cats rarely or never do this. Our canine Friends seem to do this often. The condition is called COPROPHAGY, or eating one's own stool. It can be stopped with medical tests, a change in diet, and sometimes a special compound to make the stool taste bitter. Eating cat stools can be stopped by putting the litter box where Fido cannot reach it.

GENERAL IDEAS: If you're canine friend vomits once, give him or her dose of Pepto and wait for further developments. If your feline friend vomits, give him or her some cat laxative or margarine and wait. If the vomiting continues, or has blood in it, call me. The same instructions are for the other end when diarrhea occurs. Grass eating, gurgling stomach or intestines, or tenderness in the abdomen is hyper acidity or pancreatitis and must be treated by me. I can clear up most hyper acidities by a routine of antacids that most of you have around the house. Give your friends a hug for me!! DR. Bob

Separation Anxiety In Your Friends: (Mostly Canine Friends!)

No, fellow Villagers, I am not leaving out our feline friends. However, the main sources of difficulties that can be corrected, not involving a litter box, are in our canine friends. So I will limit this article to our canine friends and their inappropriate behaviors, which primarily involve bathroom habits.

Anxiety in psychiatry is defined as a hyperactivity or increased reaction or response to a situation where there is uncertainty about the outcome or the possibility of punishment. This response becomes a house problem when the destructive behavior or inappropriate elimination (pottying in the house) is the result. And, of course, this is unacceptable to all of us. Those of you with new or young friends have experienced this house soiling and destructiveness. But I am not talking about house training. And a few of you have discovered this behavior in your long term friends who are having trouble adapting to the move to the Village. This may not be separation anxiety, but is in the same category as an inability to adapt to something new. The common link in all of these situations is that your friends have developed a very strong attachment to one or more persons in the household. They cannot stand it when you leave. Or they cannot adjust very well to changes in their environment, which is more common and easier to resolve. Simply said, you are there to help your friend through the stressful situation. The inappropriate behavior in your friend is not being spoiled, spiteful, or angry. This behavior is a distress response from your friend that he or she cannot presently cope.

A friend with any of these unacceptable behaviors must be in good medical and physical health otherwise to qualify for the behavior modification techniques and medications necessary to reverse or remove the unwanted behavior. So first, a complete physical with laboratory testing must be performed to make sure that there are no medical problems. Most of the friends that I see have a medical problem and a very few an anxiety problem. The medical problems covered in these articles over the last several months can be diagnosed with tests and a physical exam. The behavior that is left after the medical problems are resolved is what we can deal with under the dual methods of medication for anxiety and retraining.

The primary conditions that may be separation anxiety are:

1) VOCALIZATION (barking) for excessive periods of time when you are about to leave or for no apparent reason (no squirrel in sight, etc.).

2) DESTRUCTION (chewing up anything but the chewbone or rawhide) This one needs no further explanation as we all know what this is!

3) INAPPROPRIATE ELIMINATION (wetting or pooping where we are not supposed to). This presumes that there are no medical reasons for this behavior and you have eliminated those possibilities with testing.

4) EXCESSIVE SALIVATION. This one is rare, but does occur. You notice when you return that your friend has a lot of saliva on the muzzle or front legs and chest. (and there are not bad teeth or foreign objects in the mouth).

5) Tracking or circling you when you go for your coat (or golf clubs), or whatever you do in a routine manner prior to leaving the house.

6) Running wildly around, jumping up on you, and probably wetting a bit, when you return.

Any or a combination of these problems can be considered as separation anxiety.

Here are the ideas that won't work;

1) Punishment. Just makes matters worse.

2) Get a "friend" for your Friend. You are the friend. Nothing or nobody can replace you.

Here is what is recommended, possibly along with medication.

A) When you first prepare to leave the house, if that is when you see the destruction or unwelcome deposits upon your return to the house, pay no attention to your friend for 20-30 minutes before leaving. Don't talk loudly.

B) Leave a special treat or toy that you do not normally present to your friend so that this treat is only given when you are leaving.

C) When you return, ignore your friend until he or

she is relaxed or quiet. Then welcome or pet them at your own initiative.

D) Do not reprimand or punish your friend for inappropriate elimination or destruction. This will only increase the anxiety level. Of course, it won't do much for your anxiety level. But you are the one that is supposed to be doing the behavior modification.

E) Teach your friend to be calm when you move away. This may be only a few feet or another room at the beginning. Your friend must understand that you are coming back. That you are not abandoning them. Only praise calm behavior. Try to hold your tongue and your temper.

F) Most important. Put your coat on or pick up your car keys, or whatever you normally do prior to leaving several times during the day for short periods of time so that you friend will see that these items are not a sure sign that you are leaving.

G) Get a crate for time out and a simple place to put your friend in case matters are not resolved quickly. Do not feel guilty about crating (leaving your friend in a portable kennel). They do not attach any particular reason to your actions.

ABOUT THE MEDICATION YOU HAVE SEEN ON TV OR HEARD ABOUT. This medication, called CLOMICALM, is a medication that has been around for quite a while in human medicine for obsessive behavior called clomipramine hydrochloride. I have seen this medication mentioned for this use in canine behavior in books written five years ago.

Prior to this introduction, the medication was used off label. That is, it was used by veterinarians and veterinary neurologists and behavior specialists without approval for this particular use in dogs.

NOVARTIS, a very large company, has gone to the considerable expense of having the medication labeled for this particular use in dogs. The company has also gone to great lengths to develop a simple behavior modification program recommendation, which I have mentioned in this article, so that the average vet like me can work with you on a basic level.

There are very few animal behaviorists in this country and none in this area, to my knowledge. So we will try our best to help you when this drug is available under this label. It is already available in the human pharmacy as Anafranil. However, I believe that it is not very popular with human psychiatric behaviorists as there seems to be an abundance of behavior modification drugs out there for us humans. I did consult with a very highly regarded canine neurologist who indicated that he uses this medication and several others interchangeably in separation anxiety. So I have several other medications to recommend if this one doesn't work. Give your friend a hug for me! Dr. Bob

Drug Monitoring in Veterinary Medicine

I thought that I would bring you up to date on the latest recommendations in my profession of veterinary medicine regarding monitoring the effects of the medications that many "Friends" in the Village are taking. As a few of you are taking medications yourself, you know how important complete testing can be. Monitoring medications means regular testing to insure that the drug being taken on a regular basis is not doing more harm than good.

In some cases, drug monitoring will also tell you

whether the drug is working. In every case where your Friend is going to have to take medications on a regular basis, and is over six years of age, a full work up is recommended. This includes a full chemistry panel that includes electrolytes and twenty or so tests. This can be done for the same price as three or four tests done in the clinic. So they are a real bargain. The information provided in total chemistry tests is also more accurate and provides a more accurate picture of the overall health of your Friend. In every case, a complete blood count with differential should also be submitted at the same time. These base line values are very important should something go wrong in the future. Otherwise, a future elevated test would not indicate whether there was a problem before or after the medication was begun.

Thyroid Test. The most common medication dispensed to Friends is levothyroxine for a low thyroid condition called hypothyroidism. This medication is a supplement that provides thyroid hormone to the body when the thyroid glands are not producing sufficient levels of the natural hormone. Current recommendations are to have a complete blood panel and CBC test run first. If all is normal or can be explained, then once the medication has been started, recheck the thyroid hormone level after the first three weeks on the medication. Adjustments can be made at that point. Then your friend should be retested every six months.

If the thyroid test becomes elevated, a free T4 test should be run to determine if the test is high because of too much thyroid medicine or that the elevation is not a true measure of the amount of thyroid hormone available to the cells in the body. Many Friends that have elevated thyroid tests can be misdiagnosed as having too high a thyroid dose when in reality the levels are normal. Removing or reducing the medication can cause problems. Allergy medications. The commonly used steroids and antihistamines should only started after a complete chemistry 21 panel and CBC are done. These medications are not generally harmful at the levels dosed for allergy symptoms but can make other hidden diseases much worse. Long term steroid use can cause or increase the onset of

Cushing Syndrome. This condition is caused by an abnormal secretion of the adrenal glands and is very serious. I have witnessed the loss of several aged Friends in the Village to this condition. Friends on allergy medicine should be retested with full chemistry panels and a complete blood count every six months. Hyperthyroidism is cats are treated with a drug called Tapazole with some success. A Thyroid test, chest x-ray, EKG, and full chem 21 panel and CBC will confirm the diagnosis of this very serious disease. Once therapy has begun, retesting of the platelet count, CBC, T4, and chemistry panel should be done every three weeks to detect toxic effects.

Most of these kitty cats have other medical and dietary problems at the same time. Cushing Syndrome, canine pituitary hyperadrenocorticism, is very difficult to diagnose. A complete chemistry panel will provide a panorama of the functions of the body of the geriatric Friend. Since the drug of choice for treatment of this disease is toxic, a complete chemistry panel, urinalysis, urinary cortisol/creatinine ratio, CBC, urine culture and thyroid function panel should be completed first. This condition presents a complex of symptoms that can affect the tests and "shield" other underlying conditions. A low or high dose dexamethasone test is also necessary to confirm this diagnosis before beginning therapy. After the beginning of mitotane therapy an ACTH stimulation test should be done to determine the effectiveness of the therapy. The pre and post cortisol levels will indicate whether the drug is working or too much drug is being given.

Excessive dosing of mitotane can cause hypothyroidism. Phenobarbitol. This medication is used for epilepsy in both cats and dogs. It is recommended that a full chemistry, urinalysis, CBC, and blood lead test series be done before phenobarbitol therapy is begun because the drug can cause false elevations in several tests as time passes. After three weeks of phenobarbitol therapy, a trough serum level of phenobarbitol in the blood should be evaluated to see if the medication is begin metabolized properly and the dose is not excessive.

Thereafter, a complete chemistry panel and CBC should be performed every six months. Potassium Bromide. This medication is used with phenobarbitol in epilepsy therapy. So the same recommendations as for phenobarbitol should be followed and a Potassium Bromide serum concentration should be performed after the first three weeks and at four months, then every six months. Digitalis , Enacard, and Lasix. These three drugs are used to treat heart conditions. Digitalis can be toxic. Enacard is very safe, but may not be effective at the recommended dose because of liver or kidney function. Lasix is safe but can reverse the effectiveness of Enacard. An accurate diagnosis of the exact heart condition is essential before beginning any of these medications. A complete chemistry panel (21) including electrolytes, urinalysis, thyroid profile, x-rays, EKG should be done as a minimum to avoid serious complications from one or a combination of these medications. As these Friends usually have other conditions, better safe than sorry! Every three months, liver and kidney function and digitalis blood levels should be tested to insure the best results from the medications. Diethylstilbesterol (DES) This drug is an estrogen compound used primarily to treat incontinence in female doggy friends and for itching in kitty friends. A, CBC should be done before beginning therapy and repeated every three months.

Some of you will not agree to these recommendations for cost or other considerations. I am giving you the best recommendations because I believe that your friends deserve the best. These complete testing protocols will often help you to decide when it is time to stop since medicine is not an exact science. In the long run, I believe these protocols save money and a lot of unnecessary heartache. Give your friends a hug for me!

Chapter 6

Allergies in Arkansas and the Midsouth

Allergies: What Can You Do?

This article is about the dynamics of allergies, symptoms, and the basic medications to treat the symptoms. I have used this method for 29 years with a very high success rate. Owner compliance (your ability to stick with me for three months minimum) is essential to clearing all of the symptoms or reducing them to their winter level of activity, all year long. These articles are presented to you in a letter format, as I will be shortly printing these and updating them from time to time.

Dear Villager and Friend,

Your pet has been diagnosed as *ATOPIC* (chronic allergic dermatitis). This condition is an inherited inability to respond to challenges from **allergens** (particles of matter that are foreign to the animal's body) These particles can be anything from pollen to items in the food, such as gluten, the ingredient in wheat that is common in pet snack foods. When your pet's immune system does **not** respond to protect the body, then histamine is released. Histamine attaches to cells at certain sites in the body and causes one or more of the following standard responses that you can see or hear:

1) Itching
2) coughing
3) hives or swelling on the skin or redness

The most common allergens for this region in proportion to their intensity and effect on pets are:

1) Insect bites; mainly fleas and ticks and mosquitoes. The saliva from the insect is responsible for up to 80% of the reactions seen in pets. Most allergic pets are sensitized by insect saliva.

2) Pollens and particles from plants and trees. These items are small enough to be inhaled through the nose or the mouth. These allergens build up slowly in the system and are generally seasonal. However, there are different allergens in each the season of the year.

3) Intestinal parasites. Yes, they are foreign protein also and do have a slight contributory effect to the allergic reactions of your pet. Your pet can have parasites with a negative test.

4) Food. Direct food allergies are rare. Most animals are not directly allergic to foods. If they were truly allergic to certain foods, they would probably have bloody diarrhea within thirty minutes to an hour of ingesting the food to which they are truly allergic. For the most part, some foods are contributory to the other symptoms in your friend. Some foods simply trigger itching or make it harder to clear up allergy symptoms. The quality of your pet's food can be one of the reasons that you are having difficulty in clearing the symptoms. There are no hypoallergenic

commercial foods. They simply contain less allergen than other commercial foods. The filler added to commercial foods is generally responsible for the triggering effect.

HISTAMINE: The cause of the itching response in your pet is a product produced naturally in the body called histamine. The release of this element into the circulation prepares your pet for an itching, coughing, sneezing, spell. Histamine can last as long as 2-3 weeks in the circulation. An allergic pet is producing histamine constantly, which is accumulating in the blood stream and_increasing the chances for a "triggering" of the itch response.

REDUCING HISTAMINE: DIET: No foods with wheat gluten. Change fat source about every ninety days (i.e., chicken/rice to lamb/rice to ...) No commercial diets are allergen free!

ANTIHISTAMINE/PREDNISONE : These medications will reduce circulating histamine on a long term basis.

BUG CONTROL: Frontline monthly on your Friend.

HYPOALLERGENIC SHAMPOOS/CRÈME RINSE: Weekly, approved by Dr. Bob.

EXERCISE: Makes the food and medication work better!!

Do It Yourself Biting Insect Control, Inside and Out /or :(how to live in Arkansas as if you were in Chicago!)

If you have lived in Arkansas for one full set of seasons, you have probably realized that you are; 1) living in a semi-tropical Gulf climate with ten months or more of warm weather 2) coexisting with insects who also find this weather very pleasant for reproduction 3) understanding that your friends (dogs and cats), and you under certain conditions, are very attractive as snacks for many varieties of insects here. So with that in mind I am going to give you my personal home routine for coexisting with the various biting hordes of insects in Arkansas. I have lived for the past fifteen years in both North East and South Central Arkansas, in both Delta and Mountain locations. This information works in both areas.

I put Frontline on both my dog and cat friends every month of the year. My dog goes in and out and can bring ticks in, so I don't use Advantage, because it only gets fleas. The months of November through the end of January are not tick months here although you may see an occasional one. So I consider those three months by the label on the Frontline as a time to save a little money or I use Advantage. During the warm months I spread (broadcast) flea and tick granules in the areas most used by my outside pets every two weeks. I use only Diazanon as it is presently the only granular residual bug treatment that I am familiar with and comfortable recommending to you. These granules come from the same manufacturer under many labels so the cheapest is as good as the most expensive. I do not cover the entire yard. I "band" the yard for three feet in from the fence around the entire yard and along the foundation of the house. I always treat all the way around the foundation of my house for about three feet out from the foundation to keep the ants and other critters from entering the house. I also spread some of the granules in front of the doorways to the house to discourage the fleas from jumping into the house when the doors are opened. I treat the inside of the house with a residual spray containing Permethrin or

Tetramethrin around the baseboards in each room and the kitchen once a month. Catches the mother fleas before they produce any baby fleas. The permethrin types of sprays are the best we have at this point, in my opinion. Remember that these treatments kill all insects that come in contact with them. If your house becomes infested and you want to do it yourself, the packs of household foggers work well if you do the following: 1) open all of the doors in your house to every closet, room and cabinet. 2) Tilt the couch pillows down and pull back or strip your bedspreads. 3) Set the foggers on chairs in open areas, such as a hallway, so that the fog will reach into all of the rooms. 4) Remember that fleas don't obey your house rules about which rooms they will enter. So treat them all. 5) Turn up your thermostat or turn off your air conditioner so that it will not come on during the fogging period and pull all of the fog out of your house. 6) Change vacuum bags monthly to prevent flea larva that you vacuum from hatching. This is not as frequent as their hatching period but will do if you fog, treat your house, and use Frontline on your friends.

Some friendly hints: flea dips only last three days at full strength in Arkansas on the dog or cat no matter who says what about that. Flea sprays only last three days maximum, in my experience. Flea collars are for a high-rise apartment in Chicago! Yeast is for baking bread!

Remember that we spend all of our lives seeking friends, spouses, family for unconditional love, when they have been sitting on our laps or at our feet all the time! Give your pets a hug for me! Dr. Bob

Skin Allergies in our Kitty Friends

Since excessive hair loss in our Village Kitty Friends seems to be on the rise, a review of the possibilities and the preventions would be in order. The Mysterious Feline Immune System. Our feline friends do not have the same physiology as we humans or doggy friends. They seem to have a different response to challenges by their immune system. However, their response to allergens, substances foreign to their bodies, is very simple; they scratch, groom excessively, or lose hair. Remember that allergens are substances foreign to the body.

The feline immune system produces antibodies every second of every day to neutralize these allergens. When the immune system is unsuccessful, or more often, too slow to respond, the symptoms mentioned occur in some combination. I generally notice excessive grooming first with the accompanying vomiting of hair balls. (A cautionary note to those of you feeding the new hairball medicine; you are probably masking an allergy in your friend). The more uncommon reasons for allergic dermatitis in your kitty friends are not present on the Village, in my experience; notoedric mange (a mite usually found in alley cats) cheyletiellosis (rabbit mite) notoedric mange (cat mite spreading over the skin), fur mites (Lynxacarus radovsky!! from wild animals). These are very common!! ; Fleas! fleas!, fleas!, otodectes (ear mites), trombiculosis (chiggers). Please remember that you are in Arkansas and that you cannot isolate your home from fleas or chiggers, if you ever go outside for any reason. Fleas will come into your house looking for a meal. Chiggers will attach to you (somewhere) and drop off in your house looking for your Friend or some bed sheets. Internal parasites: There are no parasite- free kitty friends outside of the laboratory. Although intestinal parasites seem to be a mild source or contributor to itching, they are still a factor. Fungus; The soil fungi are rare here, but do occur. Excessive licking over a long period of time generally opens the skin to infection or infestation by fungi. Atopy/Food Allergy; these terms are interchangeable as one tendency must be present for the other to occur.

Treatment; Reciting my mantra on this:

a) deworm once or twice annually (won't hurt them a bit)

b) feed only the highest quality foods (they will eventually eat what you give them!)

c) Seek professional help (preferably mine!) to determine the source of the allergy.

d) Frontline or the other flea control year around.

e) Treat your house once monthly May-October minimum.

Give your friends a hug for me!!

Chapter 7

Emergency First Aid at Home

Cuts, bites, and scratches. Clean the wounds with soap and water unless there is a hole into a body cavity. If there is a puncture, cover it and seal it. Apply a clean cloth or paper towels over wounds to stop bleeding. Wrap around the body with cloth or bandages. Call your veterinarian for guidance or a visit. Small scratches and cuts can be cleaned and disinfected with hydrogen peroxide and rubbing alcohol. Follow up with an antibiotic ointment. Cuts and scratches will heal normally within ten days or less. Protect wounds from scratching, licking, or biting by your pet. How to tell if the injury is serious.

1) Rapid or shallow breathing; panting or barely breathing at all-Check for an injured airway or damage to the mouth (Be careful. Your pet may bite you from pain or fear.

2) Pale gums.

3) Unable to recognize you or come to you.

4) Trembling or limp.

5) Temp below 100F or above 104F (if you have a rectal thermometer).

6) Slobbering

7) Bleeding from ears, nose or genital parts. Slow bleeding is generally from the veins and can be easily stopped by pressure. . Pulsing or squirting bright red blood is from the arteries and requires a compression bandage over the bleeding site, until you reach your veterinarians' office.

8) Broken, dislocated bones; Look over the surface of your pet for any possible breaks or bones sticking out of the skin. Try to isolate the injured area and keep your pet from struggling until you go to your veterinarian.

The three cardinal rules for emergency first aid: Stabilize, immobilize, and transport. Wrapping your Friend in blankets or bath towels is a good idea. The wounds or cuts are contaminated already. Simply use clean cloths or blankets.

Shock: This condition is the result of a reduced volume of blood flowing through the veins and arteries of the body. The gums in the mouth will be pale. If you see this, hurry to a vet. You can wrap your friend in a blanket to conserve body heat. Call for help and advice if you can. Give your Friends a hug for me! Dr. Bob

Foreign Body-Did He/She Eat it or Not?

Missing a button, thread, needle, toys, keys, etc., etc... We have all experienced this at one time or another. The esophagus of a cat can swallow up to the diameter of a penny...successfully! A doggy can swallow just about anything. If in doubt, get an x-ray before inducing vomiting. That can be terminal, you know!! If your Friend has swallowed something organic and digestible, eventually, then you can simply use the soft center of white or wheat bread to surround a suspected sharp object, or give some Pepto or Mylanta to soothe a soon to be irritated stomach wall or pylorus. Egg white does move things through more quickly if you can get the slimy stuff down the hatch!! I don't recommend peroxide to induce vomiting as it doesn't always work and can make matters worse. If the FB (or, Foreign Body) cannot be expelled in either direction, then and endoscope can sometimes remove it. We can arrange for that.

SALICYLATE (ASPIRIN) TOXICITY: The Hidden Drug

I have had several calls in the last month regarding the use of aspirin in dogs and cats. So here is the latest on that matter. Salicylates are salts or esters of salicylic acid. This is called aspirin. The main use of aspirin is for analgesia and reduction of fever in humans and animals.

This is probably the most widely used medication in the world. Due to the low cost of salicylate, however, they are incorporated into some surprising places. That is where the surprises can come!! Other than in traditional tablet form, you may find aspirin in; cold medicines, anti-fungal preparations, shampoos, wart removers, and Pepto Bismol. So, always check your labels if you are giving a home remedy to your friends.

Pharmacology; Aspirin is slowly absorbed into the body from the intestinal tract. In certain disease conditions, mainly involving the liver, the aspirin can become concentrated beyond what you wanted. The liver is the primary organ to metabolize, or use up, the aspirin. Since most of our senior doggy friends have impaired liver function to some degree, caution is in order.

To date, aspirin is not recommended for our kitty friends. They have a high degree of toxicity from this product. Effects on the blood. Long term use of aspirin can contribute to anemia in our friends. We are all also aware of the bleeding problem with long term use of aspirin. Our doggy friends can take this product for a long time, but clotting or prothrombin times should be checked regularly to avoid any real problems. Dosage in our canine friends; Specialists in this area of vet medicine recommend .15 grains per kg (2.2lbs is one kg), or 10mg/kg. (Some bottles still list the tablet or liquid strength in grains vs. milligrams.

Our kitty friends do not metabolize aspirin very well at all. So I do not recommend aspirin for cats under any conditions. Toxicity; Doses of aspirin at the toxic level will probably cause twitches and depression at the same time. Your unfortunate friends will exhibit all of the bizarre behavior of an animal with encephalitis. Death is usually do to respiratory or heart failure.

Treatment: Give an emetic (make them vomit) if the aspirin has been consumed within about an hour.

2) Activated charcoal can be given to absorb the aspirin left in the digestive tract and hold it for elimination

3) Wash out the stomach with sodium bicarb, presuming there is any amount of aspirin left in the stomach.

4) Blood test for acid-base determination

5) If acidotic, treat with intravenous sodium bicarbonate (this is the vet's job!)

6) Further treatment at the vet may included diuretics, vitamin K therapy for bleeding, sedatives for the convulsions and correction of dehydration.

I can tell you from experience that our doggy friends can usually be saved, but our kitty friends are rarely saved. Fortunately our kitty friends do not like aspirin and rarely ingest them voluntarily. Give your friends a hug for me! Dr. Bob (Dr. Bob can be reached at clinic 9845045 or 9224649 day or night)

Chapter 8

Nutrition

Nutrition: You Are What You Eat?

Now that you are settled into Paradise, or, the Village, as we call it, you may have discovered that you have a substantial amount of.....Time. Now you can do all of the things that you have planned for years during your trials and tribulations. The path to the Village has not been an easy one for you or your spouse. So what does this have to do with your loyal Friend who has been with you for part of those "years"?

Feeding time and frequency can now become a pleasure or a problem. Exercise will now become more important because your Friend has a few years on the body (you too!). Any Friend that is over 8 years, whether doggy or kitty cat, should have the amount and opportunity for eating brought to some reasonably regulated times. Open feeding will probably end up with acid reflux because the household routine is not a routine any more. The "mid-years" for your Friend also bring about changes in digestion and digestive efficiency. The more complex foods such as meat are more difficult to digest. The store shelf foods are generally lower in quality along with their price. There is nothing wrong with cooking for your Friend, as long as you check with me first. I can help you develop some recipes for health and happiness. A happy tummy is a healthy tummy! Quote me if you wish. Regularity in both exercise and feeding times is the formula for success.

Remember that your Friend ages approximately seven times faster than you do. You may not feel that way. But Science rules in this case. I have found that two feeding "opportunities" or times per day work for just about any situation. Very few Friends are self-controllers when it comes to food. No Friend has ever starved on the Village. Friends under 5 years can generally eat any commercial diet. If they cannot, you will soon discover little piles of white foam, yellow slime, or undigested food around your Dream House. An early warning will be the little "gurgling intestines". Take heed. I have seen a lot of white carpet with free-form yellow designs in my house call travels. Of course, you can always cover these spots with authentic Persian carpets!

Chapter 9

Silver Seniors

The majority of canine and feline Friends in the Village grow into their "golden years". This phenomenon only occurs because of the constant, loving attention accorded these fine and faithful Friends by their Villager Parents. This chapter is dedicated not only to our "Silver Senior Friends", but to their Villager Senior Parents!!

"Silver Seniors"- Rover's Turn!

This puppy dog is ten years old. He moved to the Village with his parents sans children. He lives in a fine house that is exceptionally quiet compared to the Old Life. Oh, the Kids visit once in a while with some new Little Kids that Rover has never seen. They are enjoyable. They even look a little bit like his Kids. So he accepts them, probably plays a little bit with them. He, like Mom and Dad are sorry to see them leave, but do welcome the rest and return to a quiet house again. Rover has his favorite foods. He likes Dibbles and

Bits, Gravy Train, and of course, Also and Mighty Dog. Real red-blooded All American foods that a dog can sink his teeth in to. However, since he has moved to the Village, he has begun to itch a little. He also occasionally wakes up with an acid stomach and has to go outside to sneak a few blades of grass when Mom and Dad aren't watching him. Rover hasn't had this much attention in his entire lifetime. Mom and Dad watch him constantly. They are always around, for some reason. Why, he can't even have a quiet moment to throw up behind the bushes outside!

Rover's eyes are also becoming a bit cloudy. He can still see very well. This condition is a normal aging process called nuclear sclerosis. Rover also has these little brown things attaching to him (ticks) and occasionally something invisible bites him like crazy! (chiggers). He has to wear that "smelly stuff" on his neck all year now. There is no real winter here. Just a little cold snap once in a while.

Everyone here is very nice to him. They all say hi! when he is out for his walks. And Mom and Dad are really getting into this walking. Rover has to take this treat once a month to keep away the "heart worms", whatever they are. He has had a few mosquito bites. He really can't remember mosquitoes back in the Old Life. They were probably frozen or chilled most of the time and couldn't bite very well! Mom and Dad seem really worried about this throwing up. So I won't do that when they are watching. However, if I don't, I get diarrhea. Of course, I pick the white carpet because it seems like the best place to do this. Mom and Dad just had a "vet" come over to the house. He seems nice. Smells very interesting. He gave Mom and Dad some food for me to eat and some little pills. Anyway, I don't itch any more. So I feel better. I don't feel like throwing up any more either. And I am losing some of my "love handles". This Village Life is a pretty good deal! Give your friend a hug for me! Dr. Bob

Cholesterol and Your Senior Friends. We Villagers are all familiar by now with "good" and "bad" cholesterol and the long term effects of both kinds. If you are not as yet familiar with these terms, just wait another ten years and you will become an expert. We all watch our cholesterol in the foods we eat. Judging from the many surgical scars I see down at the Nat, quite a few of you are now on restricted cholesterol diets. Our canine and feline friends, as they age, can develop some problems with cholesterol. They can even experience "hardening of the arteries" (atherosclerosis). In the last three years I have seen an increased interest in those conditions in our aged friends. So here is the very latest in both canine (dog) and feline (cat) veterinary internal medicine on the subject.

Lipids. These are the fats in your friends' systems that are necessary for the normal functions of the body. These lipids (fats) come from the fats in your friends' meals. These fats cross through the intestinal wall into the bloodstream in various forms after being digested. These fats are either stored as fat (hopefully, not to excess!) or used as energy. (Walks after meals can shift more to this use). There are two basic categories of fats, triglycerides and cholesterol.

Triglycerides are the most abundant type of lipid in dogs and cats and are called VLDL, Very Low Density Lipoprotein. A portion of these are further broken down into LDL, Low Density Lipoprotein.

Cholesterol is used for energy transport in the cell membranes and is needed for hormone production, vitamin creation (in your canine friends) and bile acids (used in digestion). Cholesterol is called HDL or High Density Lipoprotein. Both types are needed for energy processes. The processes which use them are complex and detailed beyond the space in this article. Simply said, they are very necessary, in essential amounts, for the normal functioning of the body. In humans, the LDL is more important. In our canine and feline friends, HDL is more important (factoid).

An excess of fat in your friends' bloodstream is called hyperlipidemia, or high amounts of fat. This condition occurs normally after each of the one or more meals and fatty treats of the day. Of course, a high amount of fat in the system cannot all be utilized or stored immediately, so it circulates. If a blood sample is drawn after a meal (post prandial), your friends' blood sample will have a layer of fat in it that looks like the cream that used to be on milk. This is called primary or postprandial hyperlipidemia. (I did not make this up) A blood sample drawn from your friend after a twelve hour fast should have no fat in it. If it is lipemic (fat-containing), it may indicate a medical problem. If the high fat level is due to a disease, it is called secondary hyperlipidemia. Diseases that can cause a fasting blood sample to contain a significant amount of fat are; diabetes mellitus (sugar diabetes) in both your feline and canine friends. In your canine friends only; hypothyroidism (low thyroid hormone), hyperadrenalcorticism (Cushing disease), and protein-losing nephropathy (filtering or absorbing deficiency in the kidney). There also appears to be a correlation between long term obesity in your friends and hyperlipidemia, leading to one of the above conditions.

Of course, we vigilant Villagers who read our medical articles all know that being overweight and not exercising enough can lead to most of these conditions. So common sense tells us that the same can occur in our friends. There is also a connection between friends that have recurrent pancreatitis, usually from food intolerance or overeating, and hyperlipidemia. It is also possible that high levels of fats in the body from overeating for years can produce pancreatitis. However, I believe the most common cause of pancreatitis to be simply from indigestion rising from overeating or eating the wrong foods.

You may remember that the pancreas contributes to the proper breakdown or digestion of the fats in the meal. An overworked or under-producing pancreas can ultimately be damaged by high fat levels in the blood over a long period of time. There are some very rare inherited causes of this disease. More common is the occurrence of hyperlipidemia in miniature schnauzers, generally in later life. Veterinary researchers have not discovered the exact cause of this, but it is quite common in older miniature schnauzers.

You may not observe any symptoms in your friends from this disease in the early stages. Normally, the condition is discovered during routine blood tests. Rarely, a condition of fat globules in the eye sometimes is seen during an eye exam (lipemia retinalis). A very rare lump on the skin (xanthoma) can occur. Seizures and disorientation can also occur from excessive fat in the bloodstream. Atherosclerosis or hardening of the arteries can occur. This condition would only be diagnosed at autopsy. So what can a Villager do to avoid this condition in your friends? Watch the calories and the fats. There are some new and very fancy low cholesterol diets.

The simplest one substitutes soy protein for animal protein. The lowering of the blood fat level seems to help. There is a liquid/powdered liver "booster" supplement that helps a lot. Exercise as much as can be tolerated. I realize that many of our golden seniors (our friends) cannot take long walks anymore. Any exercise will help. Annual checkup and blood tests catch problems early. Very simple. Common sense. Very easy to do. Give your friends a hug for me.

When Your Friend Starts to Wobble or Stagger

I have just finished reviewing my article of 9/98 concerning the brain and its functions. Since there has been a rash of "wobbling" doggy and kitty Friends through here lately, I thought this would be a good time to review some things you can look for.

Old Friends: The middle ear in our friends is responsible for normal balance. The little hairs in the fluid in the bulla (little container) move with movement and send signals through the brain to the limbs to balance. When any interruption anywhere in this system takes place, your Friend will stagger or fall over. The difference between this type of staggering and a seizure is the intensity of a seizure. Also, middle ear problems are repeat problems. Seizures will not recur that frequently. Seizures also last longer. Your friend will not recognize you until the seizure are over.

Wobbling from a concussion can be confused with a middle ear problem. However, a concussion will usually affect the dilation of the pupils. One pupil will react to light more slowly than the other. Uneven pupil dilation is evidence of pressure or trauma to the brain. A slow-growing brain tumor will eventually cause staggering.

Head tilt: Most middle ear problems affect one side more than the other. So your Friend will tilt the head more to one side or the other. Any other persistent wobbling is from the brain down the spinal cord. Any interference or injury along the way can cause wobbling or uneven gait. These conditions, unless caused by sudden trauma, do not usually improve. Give your Friends a hug for me!! Dr. Bob

Skin, Bumps, and Lumps. To Freeze or Not To Freeze. That is the Question!

Our Senior Friends population occasionally develops lumps and bumps. There are several types that are common. Cysts: These bumps are generally smooth to the touch. They don't hurt when you squeeze them. They feel like they are filled with fluid. They generally come up rather fast. Most of the small breeds and their crossed-bred brethren develop these. We vets don't really know why. Some of these cysts develop a cheesy exudate (discharge) that comes out on to the skin surface. These are called sebaceous cysts. They are not harmful. If they become large and will not reduce on their own or with a little help from your friendly vet, then they can be surgically removed.

Squamous Cell Carcinoma. This bump is a real

tumor. They are quite rare in our friends. However, lately in cats, they have been identified more frequently. Probably because our Friends are living much longer (good food and lots of love). They should be removed by surgery.

Epithelioma: This bump is very common in our poodle ancestry Friends. They appear everywhere. They are easily frozen with cryosurgery. This is a method of freezing just like the method used on humans. And to think we used to call those "beauty marks"!

Mast Cell Tumor: These bumps develop in areas that have been irritated or agitated. I have seen many develop where a "worry spot" or "itch spot" has been for a long time. They can also be frozen under certain conditions.

Melanoma: These are the tumors we all worry about on our bodies. They do occur frequently on our canine friends. I don't believe that I have ever seen one on our feline Friends. They are black bumps. If they are small, they can be frozen first. Some will want them surgically removed. Unlike our human melanomas, they don't seem to metastasize (spread) very much. So the outcome is not as serious as in humans.

Cryosurgery: This technique is very common now with the development of disposable cans of liquid nitrogen. The freezing technique basically applies this super cold spray to a bump. The bump is frozen entirely. The "ice ball" that forms hurts a little bit because it is a frost bite. But the pain is transient and far safer than general anesthesia. The bump will turn black in a few days. Generally the bump will then fall off, leaving a healthy red spot where new skin will grow. If the bump does not freeze completely, then we refreeze the bump. Stubborn bumps can then be removed by surgery. I would suggest that you simply have any bump that interferes with the grooming clippers or aggravates your Friend removed, if possible, by cryosurgery. Give your friends a hug for me! Dr. Bob

Cancer in Dogs

Since our Friends are living much longer in these times, cancer is a much more common occurrence. Our doggies Friends in the Village have their share of these problems. Most are treatable. Remember that cancers still occur infrequently.

SKIN TUMORS: The most common skin tumor, the epithelioma, is comes with old age. Primarily found in the small breeds. The tumors are generally benign. I remove them when they interfere with the groomer's clipper or when they aggravate your Friend or you. Unspayed doggies do occasionally develop mammary tumors. The tumors in the breast area generally mean the uterus is also cancerous. If they are both removed, the chance of recurrence is small.

FATTY TUMORS (LIPOMAS). These tumors are quite common. They are soft and painless. Some stop growing and start to enlarge. They are removed when they become a problem to the doggy.

FIBROMA/FIBROSARCOMA. These are the hard skin tumors that you can generally feel. They are usually encapsulated (self contained in a capsule) and are removed as they occur. Some can be malignant.

LYMPHOMA-SARCOMA: The lymphoma-lymphosarcoma group of tumors occurs most frequently in small breeds of aged doggies. There is a skin (cutaneous) form and a nodal (lymph node) form, and an internal form. This particular tumor has been treated successfully with small dose chemotherapy. Otherwise, it is fatal.

A fairly common surface tumor, a HISTIOCYTOMA, can result from an old injury, or a gum inflammation. This tumor is usually cherry red and can be highly neoplastic (spread rapidly). The gum tumors are generally fatal. There are some benign gum and tooth tumors. Asyour Friends age, an annual exam will usually detect tumor formation early. Treatment: Cryosurgery; I freeze most small tumors or remove them surgically and freeze the area. Even tumors in the mouth can be treated and reduced in this manner. I always recommend histopathology (test the tumor tissue) as we do occasionally get a surprise result.

Cancer in Cats

This article is follow-on to last week's article on Canine Cancers .Lymphoma: Remember that any disease that affects the bone marrow system of your friend can result in an abnormal production of cells, in this case lymphocytes. These cells are a product of the immune system of the body. They are involved in round the clock protection of the body. An excessive amount of lymphocytes in the blood generally signals that an attack is on.

Under normal conditions the body routinely removes billions of unnatural cells every day. However, when there are a lot of unnatural cells being produced, one may slip through that the body's defenses cannot remove? That cell is called a cancer cell. A cancer is simply a cell that the body cannot eliminate in time to prevent damage. Since viruses and the disease symptoms they cause are quite common in our feline friends, a condition called lymphocytosis can occur quite readily. The word lymphocytosis means many, many lymphocytes above the normal amount in the body.

I have seen many feline friends develop this condition after a virus. Many of these lymphocytosis conditions are resolved by a healthy immune system. I am sure that many of these conditions go undetected because our feline friends don't always act sick. Generally, however, a prolonged attack of this kind results in a mass growing somewhere on the body. Most lymphoma is first discovered by the presence of an enlarged lymph node or a singular mass on the body, which is not painful. The mass must be biopsied to accurately diagnose this disease. The other normal symptoms of illness such as lethargy, inappetance are not diagnostic of this condition. These could be normal Village behaviors for our pampered feline friends!

Now that you understand that a challenge to the immune system produces the conditions for the cancer of the lymph system called lymphoma, you may remember that Feline Leukemia virus, Feline Immunodeficiency virus, and any other virus that attacks the immune system of your friend could result in lymphoma. So lymphoma is not generally considered a primary condition.

Those unfortunate feline friends that are not routinely vaccinated against leukemia and FIP (feline infectious peritonitis) often develop lymphoma secondarily. So a simple vaccine program can reduce the possibility of this disease. Incidentally, I have seen that feline friends, who test positive to feline leukemia virus, after two tests of course, are generally positive for one or more of the other feline diseases. This is probably due to a weakened immune system. Treatment: The drugs used to treat feline lymphoma are the same as those used for humans. The side effects and prognosis are just as guarded. Our feline friends do not seem to have as much trouble with vomiting. Please remember that your feline friend is aging about seven times faster than a human. So the long term predictions for successful feline lymphoma patients are 3-6 months. Please give your friends a hug for me! Dr. Bob

Tumors

The most common tumor in kitty cats was mammary carcinomas in unspayed female cats. However, since responsible Villagers spay their female cats, very few of these tumors have been observed. The skin tumors and mouth tumors in our kitty Friends are the most common but still very rare. The skin fibroma and the fibrosarcoma, the first benign and the second malignant do occur here. Fatty tumors seem to occur infrequently in our kitty Friends. Out kitty Friends do develop blood cancers called dyscrasias, where one or more types of cells in the blood system go out of control. Leukemia is the most common. Our Kitty Friends develop just about every type of cell cancer that we humans do. Treatment: Removal or freezing are the best methods for anything that can be felt or seen. The cellular or blood cancers respond to chemotherapy but the kitty Friends do not. The thyroid tumors that seem to be frequent in our geriatric kitty Friends do respond to radio isotope therapy quite well. There is a recovered kitty Friend that moved here recently. This treatment is quite expensive but successful.

Surgical removal of thyroid tumors in kitty Friends is not very successful. Lipomas. Our kitty Friends do occasionally develop these. We usually dissect them if they become uncomfortable or interfere with our kitty Friends quality of life. Histiocytoma: This cherry red tumor sometimes will develop from a chronic irritation or old scar area. I have removed a few of these. They are considered malignant. The ones around the mouth and lips do not respond very well to treatment.

Nutrition in Skin Conditions: "You are what you eat!"

Doggy and kitty friends require energy, amino acids, fatty acids, glucose precursors, vitamins, and minerals for growth and maintenance. I will focus on the skin since that is the most sensitive and first organ of the body that will show deficiencies in diet, or many diseases for that matter. Other than allergies, which are rampant in Village Friends, the diet is the usual source or reason for dry coats, flaky dandruff, dull coats, and poor hair coats. Presuming that your friend is able to absorb nutrients, if they are present in adequate amounts in the food, then only what is in the diet can be absorbed and used.

Protein and Amino Acids: These protein sources that come from food are necessary to build the proteins that produce skin and hair. Protein is used best when adequate amounts of fats and carbohydrates. Careful readers of my previous article will note that our friends do not have the problems with fats that we do, excepting obesity. Protein and/or calorie malnutrition results in thin, weak, or fragile hair that easily falls out. A dry dandruff is also usually present (presuming there is no disease or allergy present).

Fat: Fat in the diet provides energy. Fat is a complex of saturated and unsaturated fats, very similar to our systems. Our doggy friends can convert linoleic to linolenic and arachidonic acids, which is only important because we humans can also do this. Our kitty friends cannot convert linoleic acid so they require all three of these fatty acids in their diet in a prepared form (meat, fish, and egg products in prepared cat foods). Fat deficiencies, (hardly a problem here!) result in the same scaly coats, thin hair, hair loss, etc...

Vitamins: The B vitamins are essentials to many processes in our friends. Deficiencies in any of the B vitamins results in many obvious and some hidden problems. All prepared pet commercial and prescription diets have these vitamins added in adequate quantities. However, please remember that these vitamins are not completely stable and do degrade over time. Fresh food or preserved food is essential to keeping up the vitamin content. Supplementing your friend's diet without consulting with a vet can eventually become a problem. I have seen very little problems in the Village with improper supplementation. Vitamins A, D, and E: These fat soluble vitamins are even more unstable. They must be present in adequate amounts for normal metabolism, especially calcium metabolism.

Minerals: The major or macro minerals are calcium, magnesium, potassium, sodium, chlorine, phosphorus, sulfur. The trace or micro minerals are chromium, copper, iodine, manganese, nickel, silicon, vanadium, cobalt, fluorine, iron, molybdenum, selenium, tin, zinc. These elements are the obvious minerals. There is increasing research into obscure minerals as the profit motive drives the pet food industry. Before you embark on a home remedy vitamin or special supplement to cure a dry skin, please call me for a review. Look before you leap! Your friend deserves no less!! Please give your friend a hug for me. Dr. Bob

Chapter 10

Wellness and Good Health

Laboratory Testing: When and what for?

Our aged feline Friends are generally the most frequently tested patients on the Village. They seem to hide their conditions and symptoms the most. Our canine Friends can act out their discomfort better. Lack of appetite and/or lethargy in our feline Friends is often very confusing. And I must add, fellow Villagers, that drawing blood from our feline Friends can be quite exciting! The blood and urine tests for your kitty Friend are generally the same as the human tests. However, the values and results are a bit different.

Serology: These tests are run on the serum that is separated from the blood. These tests are based upon changes in average values for certain enzymes or waste products that are produced by the body. Since the tests are based upon products found in the serum, they are termed serum chemistries. When the tests are higher or lower than what are considered normal values, they are interpreted by the veterinarian. Since there is rarely only one test that is high or low, giving a combined interpretation is the challenge. The most predictable serum chemistries in our feline Friends are BUN (blood urea nitrogen), creatinine, and SGPT (Serum glutamic pyruvic transaminase). In fact, these tests are fairly predictable in our doggy Friends and in we humans also.

BUN: The body produces urea as a by-product of protein digestion. Urea is considered a waste product. The kidney very predictably filters this waste product from the body. When an inflammation of the kidney occurs, this value goes up. It can come back down. However, an old tired kidney will not filter urea very well either. If the feline is not digesting protein or eating enough protein, the urea value will be very low. Urea in high concentrations is toxic to the body and can cause severe symptoms.

Creatinine: This enzyme is produced in the body and very predictably filtered by the kidney. Most veterinary clinical pathologists agree that this value rarely exceeds normal unless more than 60% of all functional kidney tissue has been lost due to disease or age. This test value often will not go down very much simply because it is primarily a function of living healthy kidney tissue.

SGPT: This test is considered an active evaluator of liver function. Almost any dysfunction of the liver will elevate this test. An elevated SGPT is almost always accompanied by several other liver enzymes tests that will be elevated. Since it is considered an indicator of inflammation in the liver, it can go down to normal levels. In advanced liver disease, it rarely goes back down.

Amylase: This test is a bit controversial. The enzyme is not specific for the pancreas but is often elevated in the presence of an inflammation of the pancreas. However, pancreatitis is being diagnosed and successfully treated on the Village. There are 21 chemistries commonly run together in our feline Friends to give the veterinarian a complete picture of organ function and health or disease in the body. Reducing inflammation with medication and generally changing the diets to a higher quality are the two standard methods for reducing these test values toward normal. Please remember, fellow Villagers, that diet. is everything in our feline Friends? Read the labels please! And give your friends a pat or hug for me! Dr. Bob

Vaccinating your Friend in the South

Your Friends can catch these common contagious diseases in the Village because the wild animals that live here carry these diseases. Raccoons can carry both feline and canine distemper. Foxes carry Fox Hepatitis, which is in the common canine vaccine. Bobcats, wild cats, and lynx can carry all of the feline diseases. Coyotes carry all of the canine diseases. Skunks carry rabies but do not necessarily die from the disease. Raccoons, foxes, coyotes all can carry rabies. Fellow Villagers and Friends! We are not alone!!

Feline Distemper, Leukemia, AIDS, Infectious Peritonitis

Feline Distemper
This is the most common viral disease in cats. The virus actually causes a panleukopenia, which means that the white cell count in the blood test is very low.

This disease is very common in cats that were not vaccinated early in life against the disease. The virus is resistant to most disinfectants. The virus is also carried by raccoons, ferrets, and mink. The virus is transmitted directly in the secretions of the feline body, especially the feces (stool) or (diarrhea). The virus can attack all parts of the body, so the symptoms can be multiples. Most cats that have the disease act dizzy or depressed. They usually run a high fever. Recovered cats sometimes have "twitches" or stagger a bit. Many have loose stools or are always having runny stools. Many older cats that had a touch of distemper when they were kittens and recovered will sometimes have a return of the symptoms when they are much older. There are cats that recover from the virus and then carry the virus, periodically shedding the virus in their stools. There are other diseases with these symptoms. The vaccine is very effective in preventing the disease.

Feline Leukemia

This disease in cats is similar to the disease in humans. There are no possible ways for humans to get leukemia from cats. Humans that have been accidentally sprayed with the virus have not developed the disease. Because the virus that causes leukemia in cats has been isolated, a vaccine has been developed that has been effective. Infected cats become anemic. They eventually die from complications of anemia. Some cats recover in some form while other cats can carry the virus and not die from it. There are very accurate tests for the leukemia virus. There are probably different carrier forms of the virus that have not been identified as yet. I have never seen leukemia in a vaccinated cat.

Feline AIDS.

Yes, Villagers, there is an HIV virus for cats. This particular name describes a type of virus similar to human HIV, but not the same. There is a test for this virus that is fairly accurate. The test is done in large laboratories. There is no vaccine for this virus as yet on the market. The symptoms in cats are the same as in humans in that the virus attacks the immune system of cats causing other symptoms from bacteria to appear. There does appear to be cross immunity to this disease. A high percentage of cats that contract leukemia or other viral diseases eventually develop this disease also. So the virus is considered to be an "opportunist" virus in that it attacks a weakened immune system. I have not seen this disease by itself except in non-vaccinated cats.

Feline Infectious Peritonitis

This disease is nearly always fatal. It exists in two forms in cats. The "wet" or effusive form results in liquid developing in the abdomen of the cats. This is the acute form that we usually see. Treatment is rarely successful. The "dry" or non-effusive form is a very slow progression. Dry lumps develop in the abdomen. The disease is commonly transmitted by saliva. Some cats evidently do recover. They are usually the ones vaccinated against the other diseases. There is a new vaccine to help in preventing the disease. There also seems to be cross-immunity here. Please remember that vaccines are not perfect but much preferred to the alternative of not vaccinating. Playing roulette with your cat's health is not a good idea. Immunity decreases as your friend ages.

THE FUTURE: Much research is being done in recombinant immunizations. These products will prevent diseases at the most basic cell level in the body. There is a recombinant "vaccine" for cattle that is now on the market. These products do not give the disease nor contain the disease virus. So the future is looking better for our feline friends. Merry Christmas to you all! Give your friends a hug for me!

Vaccines: A Review

I have been receiving a lot of questions concerning vaccines and whether they are necessary for your pet in the Village. This whole matter of whether to vaccinate or not to vaccinate emerges within the veterinary profession also. The matter is questioned invariably by veterinary faculty members who don't have to face pet owners with animals dying from a preventable disease. So I will now tell you that I have moved here from a rural area in Arkansas where all of the diseases prevented by vaccination are still very common. I can tell you that the Village is one of the safest places in a rural state like Arkansas that you can possibly spend your lives with your friends, both cat and dog. That is, if you vaccinate your friends.

There are a lot of wild animals here; foxes, coyotes, opossums, raccoons, armadillos, wild dogs and cats (strays), an occasional bear and once last summer, possibly, a mountain lion. Wild animals and strays are generally timid. However, they can and do pass through your yards at night, and will definitely come up to your homes if you leave food outside. Several of these wild animals are cousins to your dog and cat friends or are stray dogs and cats and do carry various diseases. Most of the transmissible diseases are spread by direct contact or on "fomites". That is they pee and poop or slobber, vomit, have diarrhea on your property. You can bring disease in on your shoes. You must realize that these are very slim possibilities, but never a zero possibility. You can never, never rule out the possibility of your pet being exposed to disease in the Village, no matter how careful you are.

Canine (dog) vaccines are prepared in compound form to save your pet a few "sticks" (injections). The following diseases have vaccines or bacterins that are given by your veterinarian in various combinations. Canine Distemper, Adenovirus Type 2, Coronavirus, Parainfluenza, Parvovirus, Leptospira, Bordetella.

Distemper

This is the virus that attacks the dog's brain as encephalitis. The virus can be transmitted in aerosols or saliva or possibly tears from an infected dog. It is thought that puppies are given the virus at birth from their mothers. Puppies are also given antibodies in the colostrum to protect them from this distemper virus for the first six weeks of their lives as they nurse and possibly as long as four weeks after they are weaned. They receive the majority (@90%) of these colostral antibodies in the first nursing after birth. How about that for protection!

So the virus is always around puppies and adult dogs. There is a slow and a fast form of canine distemper. The fast form progresses in a matter of days to seizures, blue eyes, and possibly hard pads on the feet. This form can be treated with some success. The slow form starts as a cough that lasts only a short time.

Weeks or months later the dog will develop a twitch, "tick", usually in the face or head muscles. The disease generally progresses to uncontrollable seizures. There is no treatment for this form, but some dogs do survive. I must tell you that my very first German Shepherd, whom I adopted at 14 months, had one of these "facial twitches" that lasted for many years and eventually disappeared. He lived to a ripe old age of 14 years. The distemper virus vaccine contains an attenuated (de-activated) form of the distemper virus. The principle here is that the immune system of your friend develops antibodies to this harmless distemper virus so that protection will be there when or if your friend is exposed the to an active virus.. Foxes, coyotes, raccoons and stray dogs carry this virus. All of these animals are here in the Village in substantial numbers. Adult dogs may be permanently immune to distemper after one vaccination. However, your friend would be the one to disprove that. I have seen several cases over the years of house dogs that developed distemper after they missed their annual vaccinations.

Infectious Canine Hepatitis (Fox Hepatitis)

Aptly named because both foxes and coyotes do carry this virus. This virus causes a fatal hepatitis in dogs. The disease is also prevented by an attenuated vaccine made from the virus itself. I have never seen a case of this disease in Arkansas in a vaccinated dog. The disease can be spread from an infected animal in bodily secretions, vomit, possibly diarrhea. This vaccine is contained in the combination vaccination given to your dog. Protection is very good. Next week: Canine Adenovirus, Parainfluenza, Bordetella (the flu and cough diseases of dogs), and Lyme (Borrelliosis).

Give your friend a pat for me, please!

Canine Vaccines: Adenovirus, Parainfluenza, and Bordetella

The sneezing, stuffy, coughing, runny nose trio! These three parts of the routine doggy vaccine are the veterinary version of the flu shot. The good news is that your friends will not catch the "flu" from any of these immunizations. The bad news is that they will not totally protect your friend from these respiratory diseases. However, they do reduce the damage from the flu viruses.

Adenovirus

This vaccine is made from the Adenovirus. The Type 2 virus has been the latest and most effective virus used to combat the common doggy cold viruses, of which there are many (over 260 active ones at latest count). This particular virus has been a vigorous defender of your friend for many years now. The symptoms of an Adenovirus infection of the body are those of the common cold. However, the Adenovirus group can cause simple runny noses to extend, or descend into the lungs into pneumonia or bronchopneumonia.

A bronchopneumonia involves one or more lobes of the lungs of your friend. Pneumonia involves all of the lobes of the lungs of your friend. Usually the condition starts as an upper respiratory matter; sneezing, runny nose, runny eyes. Then extends into the lung fields. Pneumonia is basically fluid in the lungs that are produced faster than your friend's lung system can remove it. The fluid can be watery (easy to remove) to a degree of sticky (harder to remove), to very sticky (very hard to remove). Fluid prevents oxygen from being absorbed across lung tissue into the body. The Adenovirus vaccine is very effective at limiting the damage from the adenoviruses by preparing the defenses of your friend against such an attack on the basic cell layers of the respiratory tissues of the body located in the nose, throat, windpipe and lungs. A strong defense is your friend's best offense! Our many older Village friends are particularly vulnerable to the common cold.

These viruses may exist in your friends in a latent or harmless form, held down by the circulating antibodies in your friends system. Stress can reduce these immune defenses of the body and allow the virus to "break out" of the tissues in which it may have lived for a long time from some previous cold or flu, or some chance encounter with another canine friend. Stress to your friend cannot be completely prevented. So this annual vaccination, included in the booster your friend receives from the veterinarian, goes a long way to reducing the impact of such a virus.

Parainfluenza

This is the "easy "virus. This group of viruses causes mild cold symptoms, is self-limiting in that almost any dog can resist the symptoms caused by this disease, and is usually over in a matter of a few days. This virus is included in your friend's vaccine booster because of what is called "cross-immunity". This term means that protection from this vaccine reinforces immunity against the more deadly flu viruses, such as the Adenoviruses. This concept was first discovered in humans when the milking maids of England, who commonly developed the "pox" lesions on the hands from milking cows, seemed to have more immunity to smallpox, which was fatal. In fact, the very first vaccine for stimulating cross immunity was made from the cowpox virus. So a strong immunity to the Parainfluenza virus group can reinforce your friend's immunity to the other respiratory viruses.

Bordetella

The "cough" virus. This vaccine, given in the nose of your friend, is not a virus at all. Bordetella bronchiseptica bacteria are the prime culprits in the kennel cough symptoms that are all too common in our boarded Village friends. This particular bacteria is called an "opportunist" because it invades the lining of the throat and trachea of your friend which has been weakened by a virus attacking the cells in the lining. The secretions in the back of the throat and the windpipe contain antibodies against many viruses and bacteria. Once the cells that produce these secretions and the antibodies are damaged or destroyed in any numbers, the way is open for the Bordetella bacteria to invade and cause extremes of inflammation. The irritation causes the "honking" cough that keeps us up all night. What is coughed up or out as the case may be, is full of the bacteria, which can live for a long time in secretions. That is how your friend probably caught the "kennel cough". However, these bacteria can be around just waiting for that next attack on your friend's immune system by the next wayward respiratory virus. The "vaccine" for Bordetella is not a vaccine at all, but a bacterin. This means that Bordetellas' are ground up into a soup, strained and purified, and included along with the mixture of avirulent (neutralized) viruses in the combination vaccine that we all depend upon. An annual booster against these diseases is a necessity. Next week; the feline vaccines.

Leptospirosis

This organism is a spirochete (a squiggly parasite) that lives in the urinary tracts of rats, mice, and can be passed to or through all kinds of mammals to your Friends. However, the vaccine fraction of this organism quite often produces illness in your Friends. I have decided not to use this vaccinate in the Village simply because the chances of transmission to your Friends is very close to zero. The frequent illness from Leptospira vaccination outweighs its value as a protection from the organism.

Lyme Disease - Tick Fever

This disease is caused by a blood parasite (Borrellia) that is injected into your doggy Friends (only) by a tick. At this time, there is no other known way to contract the disease. The same condition occurs in humans. The parasite causes high fevers that come and go. Eventually your Friend may develop arthritis of some or all of the joints (polyarthritis) which is very painful. The fevers can be treated with a special antibiotic. However, they return from time to time. Prevention of this disease by a Lyme vaccine has been very successful. Occasional mild illness from the vaccine is well worth the risk versus contracting this disease. Yes, there is a vaccine for humans. Consult your MD for that one!! This condition will be covered at length in another article. Give your Friends a hug for me!! Dr. Bob

Feline (Cat) Vaccines. The Deadly Respiratory Viruses

These groups of vaccines are also combined in combination doses to spare your feline friends extra "sticks" with the vaccination needle. The viruses that these vaccines have been designed to protect your friends against are usually fatal or very difficult to treat. All of these vaccines are given on an annual basis. Please remember that the world of vaccinations is not a perfect world. The protection percentages depend upon many factors which cannot be controlled. However, compared to not vaccinating, (the risks to your friends are obvious!) these products do give very good protection.

Feline Viral Rhinotracheitis

This long name is used to describe a virus that attacks the respiratory areas of your friend from nasal passages, down the windpipe, to the lungs. Many cats also develop ulcers on their tongues, which severely reduce appetite. All surfaces in breathing system are continuous, so the virus attacks the cells that line the airways. The protective mechanisms in the airways basically create more mucous and release more antibodies to the damaged sites. However, your feline friends are very susceptible to respiratory infections. Cats that recover from this disease generally have permanent damage to one or more areas of the respiratory system. They often have permanent nasal discharge, runny eyes, wheezing, can't meow very well, asthma-like symptoms. If you have ever adopted a "wheezy" cat, it probably had a close encounter with this virus. The vaccine is most often given as an attenuated virus. That means that the virus is "disabled" so that your friend cannot develop an actual infection, or even run a fever. Your friend's immune system will hopefully produce antibodies against this virus that will circulate for about a year or more and protect against an attack by this virus. Protection with this vaccine is very good. I have not seen a case of rhinotracheitis in a vaccinated cat...ever!

Calicivirus

This virus causes a fatal respiratory infection, generally resulting in a terminal pneumonia. The virus attacks tissues along the respiratory tracts. It also attacks the lining of the mouth, producing ulcers. Cats that survive this attack sometimes develop chronic gingivitis. This seems to be a favorite place for the virus to reside as the Calici virus can be cultured from the damaged gum tissue. This damaged gum tissue never heals completely. The only resolution is to trim all of the gum tissue back to healthy tissue. The vaccine is also an attenuated virus so immunity to the disease is very good. I have seen damaged gum tissue in vaccinated cats. However, I believe that most of this damage is due to dental problems and not the Calici virus.

Feline Rhinopneumonitis (Chlamydia)

This organism causes a pneumonitis. Pneumonitis means an inflammation of the lung tissues with no excessive fluid or mucous produced. This organism is not considered fatal by itself. Chlamydia is generally blamed for degrading the immune responses of the feline so that deadly bacteria can attack the lung tissues. It attacks the same tissues from the lining of the nose down the windpipe to the lungs. The symptoms are the same for this organism as the rhino virus. This portion of the combination vaccine is simply ground up chlamydia. Protection is not complete, but much better than no protection at all.

Veterinary researchers believe that the response by the body to this chlamydia gives what I referred to in previous articles as "cross immunity". That is, the antibodies produced against this organism offer some protection against viruses. Kitty cats that contract a case of pneumonitis from this organism usually recover. Many develop permanent tearing in one or both eyes.

Chapter 11

"Buggy" Articles for the Village and Surrounding Areas

This chapter contains a collection of articles on insect control, prevention, and treatment of your home, surrounding area, and you're Friends also. Although this was written for Hot Springs Village, the information is the same for most of the Southern States.

Who are they? Fleas, Ticks, Chiggers, and Other Critters That Bite

We are not the only ones who have recognized the many benefits of the climate and environment here in these mountains. Our fellow Arkansas in the lower elevations of Arkansas is besieged by mosquitoes from June until November. The elevation here and the lack of moist bottom lands here minimize the effect of mosquitoes. However, the other biting insects really thrive here, as most of you have discovered. I will cover the basics in this article without mentioning one *genus* or *species.* If you want details like that, come to the clinic or go to the library! Most biting insects here in the village are carried into your house by your friends. Insects can find many ingenious ways to enter your house, but these solo entries are the exception, not the rule. Friends that come in and out should have some type of insect preventative on them at all times. You must realize that there is neither perfect solution nor magical insecticide out there. You just have to treat and prevent more frequently here than in the more northern climates because we are blessed with more warm months. Next week I will cover the simple treatments and preventative measures that work best here in Arkansas which I have settled with for my home, having lived in Arkansas for the last fifteen years.

Fleas

Our most prevalent biting Village insect is found on dogs, cats, and sometimes humans. The most common fleas here are the dog and cat flea. Fleas are not fussy. They will hitch a ride on just about any warm-blooded animal in their search for their primary host, the dogs and cats; better known as "friends", the saliva from flea bites is very itchy (pruritic) and contributes greatly to the "itch index" for our friends. A really hungry flea may also bite you on occasion, causing a small red bump. Fleas can live for months before they find a dinner guest. The dog and cat fleas do spend most of their time on the furry members of your household, laying their eggs on the skin and feeding on the nutrients from the blood. A female flea can lay hundreds of eggs over a period of weeks. The larvae from the eggs feed, develop for a few weeks, and then hatch into new baby fleas. Simple math and common sense will tell you that the potential for thousands of fleas can come from a few well fed mother fleas. The eggs do fall off of your friends to your floors, carpets, cushions, and bedclothes. Thorough house cleaning efforts will generally remove most of them. The eggs and larvae can be sucked into your vacuum. Empty the bags or the canisters often so that you will not spread them.

Ticks

Ticks are blood suckers. There are several varieties of ticks here. The most common ones are; brown dog tick, dog tick, and the deer tick. When ticks attach to a warm-blooded animal they generally require 3-4 days to feed and develop before they drop off the animal. The large, blood-filled ticks are females. They feed for a minimum of one week on the host. They can produce several thousand baby ticks under ideal conditions. Ticks can carry diseases for both humans and animals. Our mild weather here provides ticks with about ten months of activity.

Mites

These critters usually have a preference for a particular host but will bite you. The scabies and mange mites prefer dogs to just about anybody. However, the scabies mite has been known to bite humans. Once, and leave a red spot or two on your lap or neck or wherever your friend spends some quality time with you. The mange mite causes "red mange" only on dogs and does not bother humans. Ear mites are very common here in both cats and dogs. They are found in the ears. I imagine that all of you have seen this in your friend's ears when they were young. The Rabbit mite does transfer to cats and dogs occasionally, from the Village rabbit population. The "creeping dandruff" found, usually on stray dogs or cats, is simply a large population of this mite. They do occasionally bite humans. Mite bites leave red bumps on human skin, whatever their origin.

Chiggers

Most of us Northern transplants are familiar with chiggers from our summers around the woods and lawns. The peak times for chiggers up North are June-August. Add five more months here on the Village. Chiggers can live more than a year .These critters will hitch a ride on just about any warm-blooded animal until they find us. The most irritating of these is the bright red-orange chigger mite. I have seen quite a few of them here in the exam room.

Spiders

Spiders are very common here also. There are many varieties here in the Village. The more common ones that are known to bite are the brown recluse and the brown spider. Spider bites on your friends are not difficult to tell from other bites. They will be individual and quite swollen. Suspected spider bites on you require a quick visit to the medical doctor.

Lice

Lice are not very common here as they are easily eradicated by routine flea treatments and shampoos. The head lice found on cats is usually found in strays here. In fact, most of the heavily infested dogs and cats here are strays.

"Woles"

I have to comment on the larva of a fly called the Cuterebra fly. The fly is a big woolly insect that lays eggs on grass or other objects. The larva sticks to passing furry creatures and enter the body. Cats seem to be particularly attractive to this larva, which enters through cuts in the skin. Once there, the larva becomes quite large, creating a swelling and a small hole, through which you can observe the larva! Seem to be a lot of them around the Village in cats who go outside.

Bees, Wasps, and Hornets

They are all here in large quantities. Their bites, of course, are severe and sometimes fatal. Your friends do not seem to be as susceptible to anaphylactic reactions as humans. However, that swollen face or nose is probably a sting and needs quick treatment. The stings are most commonly found on the face, but can be inflicted just about anywhere.

Mosquito bites here are less frequent, but just as itchy as anywhere else. Mosquitoes usually pick the top of the nose on cats and dogs. They are itchy but don't swell much.

Next Week: Common sense prevention. Common sense first aid. I will cover the simple treatments and preventative measures that work best for me here in Arkansas for the last fifteen years.

"Controlling the Bugs"

Do It Yourself Biting Insect Control, Inside and Out /or :(how to live in Arkansas as if you were in Chicago!)

If you have lived in Arkansas for one full set of

seasons, you have probably realized that you are;

1) living in a semi-tropical Gulf climate with ten months or more of warm weather

2) coexisting with insects who also find this weather very pleasant for reproduction

3) understanding that your Friends (dogs and cats), and you under certain conditions, are very attractive as snacks for many varieties of insects here.

So with that in mind I am going to give you my personal home routine for coexisting with the various biting hordes of insects in Arkansas. I have lived for the past fifteen years in both North East and South Central Arkansas, in both Delta and Mountain locations. This information works in both areas. I put Frontline on both my dog and cat friends every month of the year. My dog goes in and out and can bring ticks in, so I don't use Advantage, because it only gets fleas. The months of November through the end of January are not tick months here although you may see an occasional one. So I consider those three months by the label on the Frontline as a time to save a little money or I use Advantage. During the warm months I spread (broadcast) flea and tick granules in the areas most used by my outside pets every two weeks. I use only Diazanon since it is the only residual granular insecticide left on the market; hopefully, new ones are in development, as I do find resistance to Diazanon.

These granules come from the same manufacturer under many labels so the cheapest is as good as the most expensive. I do not cover the entire yard. I "band" the yard for three feet in from the fence around the entire yard and along the foundation of the house. I always treat all the way around the foundation of my house for about three feet out from the foundation to keep the ants and other critters from entering the house. I also spread some of the granules in front of the doorways to the house to discourage the fleas from jumping into the house when the doors are opened. I treat the inside of the house with a residual spray containing Permethrin or Tetramethrin around the baseboards in each room and the kitchen once a month. This method catches the mother fleas before they produce any baby fleas. The permethrin types of sprays are the best we have at this point, in my opinion.

Remember that these treatments kill all insects that come in contact with them. If your house becomes infested and you want to do it yourself, the packs of household foggers work well if you do the following:

1) open all of the doors in your house to every closet, room and cabinet.

2) Tilt the couch pillows down and pull back or strip your bedspreads.

3) Set the foggers on chairs in open areas, such as a hallway, so that the fog will reach into all of the rooms.

4) Remember that fleas don't obey your house rules about which rooms they will enter. So treat them all.

5) Turn up your thermostat or turn off your air conditioner so that it will not come on during the fogging period and pull all of the fog out of your house.

6) Change vacuum bags monthly to prevent flea larva that you vacuum from hatching. This is not as frequent as their hatching period but will do if you fog and treat your house, and use Frontline on your Friends.

Some friendly hints: flea dips only last three days at full strength in Arkansas on the dog or cat no matter who says what about that. Flea sprays only last three days maximum, in my experience. Flea collars are for a high-rise apartment in Chicago! Yeast is for baking bread! You can also sit back and hire one of the many pesticide companies to come and do all of this for you. They will use only safe products that will do an effective job.

Remember that we spend all of our lives seeking friends, spouses, family for unconditional love, when they have been sitting on our laps or at our feet all the time! Give your pets a hug for me! Dr. Bob
Fleas & Ticks, They are Baaack, and they bite!!!

(This is the repeat article for those Villagers who didn't get it the first time!!)

At the risk of repeating myself, and for the sake of our many new (very, very welcome!) Villagers, I am going to update and present more information on the presence and potential problems of our Village insect inhabitants. This mild Arkansas climate is also enjoyed by large volumes of insects, or critters, as we call them here. The high elevation and the lack of moist bottom lands minimize the quantities of mosquitoes here. However, biting insects really thrive here, as most of you have or will discover. Most biting insects here in the Village are carried into your house by your friends. Insects can find their own way into your house, but these solo entries are the exception, not the rule. Friends that come in and out should have some type of insect preventative on them at all times. You must realize that there is neither perfect solution nor magical insecticide out there. You just have to treat and prevent more frequently here than in the more northern climates because we are blessed with more warm months. Since tick-born diseases are the most serious, I will give you an update and an explanation on each disease.

Fleas

Our most prevalent biting Village insect is found on dogs, cats, and sometimes humans. The most common fleas here are the dog and cat flea. Fleas are not fussy. They will hitch a ride on just about any warm-blooded animal in their search for their primary host, the dogs and cats, better known as your "friends", The saliva from flea bites is very itchy (pruritic) and contributes greatly to the "itch index" for our friends. A really hungry flea may also bite you on occasion, causing a small red bump. Fleas can live for months before they find a dinner guest. The dog and cat fleas do spend most of their time on the furry members of your household, laying their eggs on the skin, and feeding on the nutrients from the blood. A female flea can liehundreds of eggs over a period of weeks. The larvae from the eggs feed, develop for a few weeks, and then hatch into new baby fleas. Simple math and common sense will tell you that the potential for thousands of fleas can come from a few well-fed mother fleas. The eggs do fall off of your friends to your floors, carpets, cushions, and bedclothes. T

horough house cleaning efforts will generally remove most of them. The eggs and larvae can be sucked into your vacuum. Empty the bags or the canisters often so that you will not spread them. The major medical problem associated with fleas is allergic dermatitis, which comes from the saliva of repeated bites. Occasionally, your friend will develop some red spots or hives from flea bites.

Ticks

Ticks are blood suckers. There are several varieties of ticks here. The most common ones are; brown dog tick, dog tick, "lone star" and the deer tick. When ticks attach to a warm-blooded animal they generally require 3-4 days to feed and develop before they drop off the animal. The large, blood-filled ticks are females. They feed for up to one week on the host. They can produce several thousand baby ticks under ideal conditions. The wild animals here are the incubators for these mama ticks. The baby or "seed ticks" go through several molting stages before they are mature and can reproduce. Our mild weather here provides ticks with about ten months of activity. In the last two weeks we have seen ticks on several patients at the clinic. Ticks can carry diseases to both humans and dogs and cats. The most common is "Tick Fever".

Chiggers

Chiggers are biters of people, not usually dogs and cats. However, your Friends are nice "transports" for bringing chiggers into your house. Awakening to little red bumps on various parts of your exterior will tell you that this is happening. Chiggers in this region of the MidSouth are not known for transmitting any disease. However, they are an aggravation. Next week. Insect-borne diseases! Dr. Bob

Lyme Disease in the Village: Dogs and People!

Since the tick season is upon us with full force, I thought it would be time to update you with the most current information on the disease and the recent introduction of a vaccine for our doggy friends. There is also a vaccine available for humans, but I will leave that up to your family doctors.

Borrelia

This little fellow is a spirochete. That means it is a squiggly-shaped organism that lives in blood. The disease is only transmitted from body to body by blood transmission. This organism lives in the blood stream of animals and is transmitted by ticks to other animals. The main carriers of Borrelia are deer ticks, which we all know, abound in the Village. Deer ticks are not particular. They will feed on deer, which don't develop the disease, but are reservoirs for the disease, and then fall off and go through their cycle of molting and growing, and conveniently hitch a ride on just about any warm-blooded critter. These ticks then attach to your doggy or kitty and have the potential to transmit the disease. Borreliosis, or Lyme Disease, doesn't seem to both our kitty friends.

At least, we vets have not connected this organism to any particular feline disease or symptoms at this point in time. However, with the introduction of a canine vaccine against Lyme Disease, you can be sure that many vaccine companies are trying to connect the disease with our kitty friends also! The deer ticks require three hosts and four different developmental steps to complete their two year life cycle. Their Spring nymphal stage and their second year Fall adult stage seem to be the two prime times. This is presuming our southern ticks are on a Spring-Fall schedule. The female ticks remain on the host (deer, mice, lizards, etc.,) for five to seven days. They then fall off, and hibernate through the winter.

Transmission to our Doggy Friends

Fall and early Spring seem to be the most likely times for transmission of the disease to our canine friends. That, in research language, does not mean that Summer and Winter are not possible infection times. That statement only means that the potential is less. Of course, these researchers are not living in the Village! Our Fall and Spring do continue for a long time around here! The information maintained by the CDC, Centers for Disease Control, on dogs indicates a very low infection rate. However, I can tell you that most of us vets don't like to talk to the government unless we have to. So I have spoken with several of the vets in the larger practices in this area and have found that those vets who routinely run titers for Lyme disease on our more blue-collar doggy friends find a very high incidence of high titers for Lyme disease. These particular doggies have a high fever and have never been vaccinated for Lyme Disease. So I believe the correlation is accurate.

Symptoms- The disease causes a transient fever, which may or may not be discovered in time. The classic symptom is a variable arthritis in our doggy friends. Signs of lameness come and go. I have seen one documented case of a recurring fever in a doggy that was tested positive for Lyme Disease here in the

Village. I know that several other doggy friends from the Village have tested positive at some of the Hot Springs vet clinics. So the disease is here.

Treatment- Antibiotics will clear up the symptoms if promptly treated. However, the disease may always be present in your doggy friend and he or she may relapse.

Prevention- At this point, only Frontline and/or a tick dip to prevent the ticks from attaching to your doggy friend can prevent the disease from being transmitted as the tick dies before it stays on your Friend for more than two days. Not very pleasant, but reassuring!!

Zoonosis- This word means, we humans can get the disease! This disease is now drawing wide interest in the medical community as possibly an under diagnosed condition. There is now a vaccine for humans against tick fever. There has been a vaccine for our doggy friends for some years now.

Vaccination- The Lyme vaccination for our doggy friends consists of ground-up (macerated) purified extract of Borrelia. This substance, when injected into our doggy friends, stimulates an antibody response, which is considered the best way to resist the disease should a tick make it past all of the defenses.

Comments: Most of the research and the attempts to diminish the potential of this disease in our doggy friends are not based upon the conditions here in the Village. I know the disease is here. The vaccine and tick prevention should prevent this from ever happening to your doggy friend. If you choose to not vaccinate against Lyme, that is your risk. Now that we know the disease can be transmitted to humans, possibly from our doggy friends, who would want to risk that after we have worked so hard to get here so we can play! Give your friends a hug for me! Dr. Bob

Erlichiosis

This disease can be transmitted by tick bites. The organism lives in white blood cells and platelets of both dogs and cats. The symptoms are what you would expect with malaria in humans; fever, depression, lack of appetite. There is no vaccine to protect from this disease. It is found in a very low percentage of dogs and cats.

Rocky Mountain Spotted Fever

This is another disease transmitted by tick bites. Both humans and dogs can catch this disease. No information indicates that it has ever been found in a cat. The organism, a rickettsia, prefers the linings of the very small blood vessels of the body where it damages them and causes hemorrhage, edema, and blood clotting. A Village Friend recently succumbed to this condition. There is no vaccine to prevent this disease.

Chapter 12

Disaster Preparedness for the Village

This article was submitted to the Disaster Preparedness Board for inclusion in the Disaster Preparedness Plan for the Village. After the "Great Freeze of 2001", we must be prepared. If there is a substantial power outage, primarily in winter, then this plan or a modification of this plan would go into effect. I rescued and cared for many of our Friends during the Great Freeze. I have to tell you that many of your Friends talk in their sleep!! Fortunately , the power grid for the Super Center and the Village Motel are shared by both the temporary facility that I am presently using and the new site for the Pet Resort and Spa (where the old Bangkok Restaurant site).

Statement- In the event of a disaster requiring that Villagers leave their residences and be housed in POA facilities, the situation will develop as to the disposition of their Friends (cats, dogs, birds, etc...) A general plan for housing and care of the animals should be included in any shelter plans, as most Villagers will not leave their pets nor can all pets survive at homes with no power or water available.

This suggested plan will deal with the matter of an actual house evacuation to a designated POA shelter.

Each Villager should own and maintain a plastic travel kennel to accommodate one or more of their pets. These kennels should be of adequate size to house each and every animal in their home. If there is more than one pet, there should be sufficient kennels to contain them in relative comfort. Animals do not react to confinement as humans do. So small and medium kennels for cats and small to medium dogs will be sufficient. Large travel kennels should house multiple pets or a large dog. In this particular situation, large kennels should not be considered as "play centers" for example, for one cat as space is a consideration. Each Villager pet should have in supply a "disaster kit", or have ready access to all of the items needed for the kit in the form of a list of items to take with a few hours notice of an impending evacuation. These items should be available in the house in sufficient supply to maintain each and every pet in that household for one week. Minimum supplies should include but not be limited to; medications, food, bottled water, kitty litter, a toy (of course), treats flea control.

Disaster Center
There should be a designated room or area of the shelter where all of the plastic kennels can be stacked and placed in an orderly manner. Ideally there should be separate areas for dogs and cats. However, this is not a problem. The area should be near an exit so that

the doggies can be walked on a regular basis.

A plastic-lined series of containers should be handy both inside the area and outside the building for disposal of animal waste, newspaper, etc. Used printed newspaper is the material of choice for bedding in the kennels as there will probably be no facilities for laundry. If possible, there should be available a tub or janitorial sink for sponge bathing of animals that soil themselves. This janitorial area should also be available to clean the soiled kennels. A hose outside, if possible, should be available to hose down the kennels. A case of paper towels should be sufficient for a week's worth of cleanups.

Villagers who are staying at the Center should be the only individuals with pets at the Shelter. However, in case a Villager has been absent from the Village or has left the Village someone else may need to care for the pet. The Animal Welfare League should maintain a roster of volunteers to assist in the care of the sheltered pets. There may be older Villagers who are not able to adequately care for the sheltered pet.

A schedule for daily exercise, feeding times, cleanup times, etc., may be needed to maintain an orderly program and Shelter Pet Area. However, there should be flexibility in this system because Villagers and pets alike will be under some stress.

Veterinary Health Considerations

If possible, proof of vaccination by a licensed veterinarian should accompany each and every pet housed in the shelter. This requirement is for the protection of all humans and animals alike. There are a very few Villagers who may not take the best care of their pets, so this is necessary. If there is a doubt, they should be vaccinated. In the event that a pet becomes ill, Dr. Bob will minister to their needs or take them to the clinic for care. It may be necessary to give Bordetella Bronchiseptica nasal inoculations to all canine pets, if they have not had this inoculation in the past six months. Housing a lot of doggies in close quarters can cause some health considerations. Kennel cough is simply the most common and most frequent.

Play Area

If possible a designated play area should be available on a scheduled basis for exercise of the sheltered pets by their Villager parents. If the parents are not available, a qualified volunteer from the Animal Welfare League should be assigned this responsibility.

Exotics and Birds

If any Villager brings an exotic animal, such as a ferret, guinea pig, hamster, etc., or a tropical bird, there should be an area, draft-free and warm, designated for the placement of the cages or containers for these animals. The same provisions for food and water should also apply here.

Death of a Pet

This unlikely possibility should be planned for as many Village pets are quite old and cannot take stress. If a freezer is not available, the bodies should be double wrapped in plastic bags and taken to the nearest facility for storage until they can be cremated or disposed of as the Villager parents decide.

Extra Food and Supplies: Disaster Preparedness

I would suggest that the Animal Welfare League keep a ready stock of dog, cat, and bird food for the possibility of a disaster requiring confinement such as that discussed in this proposal. If they are approached on this matter, I am sure they will cooperate.

I am sure there are other matters that I have not considered.

Chapter 13

Friends and Neighbors in Passing

Our Friends live to a ripe, old age in the Village. Our constant care, dietary discipline and good medical prevention programs are the reason. Saying goodbye is never easy. But goodbye is an end that will come. These articles and poems might help you in your time of "saying goodbye".

Saying Goodbye

This is a tribute to a Friend who will not be with us much longer. Her story might give some of you pause for thought, a chance to revisit pleasant memories, and reflection. Perhaps you might also see the positive in the inevitable results that these life stories bring to all of us. I was brought into this world, one of many in a noisy, squealy, yippy pile of brothers and sisters. I know that I was selected to replace another fuzzy doggy that had graced the home and hearts of a family with children now grown and in their own homes. At first, my new parents did not really want another Friend, having grieved for that loss. That is understandable, because we puppy dogs do play a very important role in the fabric of a family. I am sure she gave many wonderful years of support and solace and companionship to mom, dad, and the little ones. She was there to lick their faces and roll around in the grass. She was there when the kids simply needed someone to talk to who would listen to them on their level. Mom and Dad were very busy raising the family and putting food on the table to take a lot of time for her. She probably was a bother at times and just another mouth to be fed. Once the house was empty and quiet and the refrigerator stayed full for the first time in years, I am sure that Mom and Dad began to see her value to them even more. I overheard that she had passed after that time. Mom and Dad realized what a help and a blessing she had been in family raising. So you can see how hard my job was going to be. I was actually found and given by a grateful son who also saw this void in his parent's life. So I did my best. And boy was this fun! They took very good care of me. Why, they worried over me like I was one of their kids! I guess I was, and still am, that special kid to them. Years passed rapidly. So many visits with little kids and big kids coming and going. Trips and vacations and so much attention. Now we live in the Village. What a place! I have all of these critters to watch and chase whenever I want. They are all a little faster than me. But, so what. They come back every day for me to chase them again. I haven't been able to scare them off with my best growls, snarls and barks. They must like it here too! And I still get to see the kids although they are looking more like Mom and Dad every time I see them. The little kids that belong to them are also getting bigger and talking more like their Moms and Dads. I don't see very well any more. I don't hear very well either or we just don't talk as much as we used to, because we have really said all that has to be said. You see, we know each other very well. There is a comfort in that .They know what I like and don't like. And I usually get my way. I am not well now. I have been going back and forth to the hospital a lot. However, now Dr. comes to see me at home, which I really appreciate. I was really getting tired of the trips. I don't have "tests" anymore either. He gave my Mom some medicine that makes me feel better. I really appreciate that. I know he understands that. I like his voice and his touch. I guess I like just about everything about this place everybody calls the Village. Well, I guess my time is coming. I don't know who my replacement will be. I hope she does a good job. My Mom and Dad really deserve a good Friend. You can never have enough friends.

When the Time Comes: Letting Go

These past few weeks have seen the passing of some very dear friends in the Village of the cat and dog variety. So I thought I would give a few words of information to those of you who have experienced this occasion and those of you for whom this matter may soon be imminent.

1) Your friend has always been there for you. You are giving up in trying to save your friend. WRONG. Your deciding to let your friend pass, when based upon medical decisions and recommendations, really leaves you no choice. It is better to make this decision when

the alternatives, suffering and increasing stress on you and/or your housemate, have not reached distressing levels.

2) You want to do all that you can. RIGHT. Remember that a grave prognosis by me or another vet, and a second opinion for reassurance, is a terminal prognosis. If there is suffering, and anxiety is suffering, then there is no need to prolong matters.

3) You want to be there for the passing. RIGHT. You should be if you feel that you can handle the situation. Please be sure to take a seat or be in an adjacent room or location.

4) You want your voice and touch to be the last thing your friend hears or feels. RIGHT. These feelings are substantial and valid. If you feel that you can handle the emotion of the moment. Your friend will know this.

5) You want to say goodbye at the moment of passing. OK. This moment is justifiable.

6) You want to know what the procedure is for this. RIGHT. In my case, I will always tranquilize your friend so that he or she will not feel any pain from the entry of the intravenous injection. There is no need for any more pain to your friend, however small.

7) What happens after passing? RIGHT. You should have a plan for burial, cremation, or special cremation. These can all be arranged. There are presently no pet cemeteries in the area that I can recommend, but I am working on this. Cremation is a sound, humane, and practical method for passing back into dust, which we will all do some day.

8) Are outward signs of grief improper? Not at all. Letting go is important. I have found that the best way to deal with this parting is to simply discuss with your

housemate or a close friend, those happy, high points in your time with your friend. You will not run out of happy memories! This I promise you! Dr. Bob

(Charcoal was a Havana Brown cat that I inherited for a veterinary bill in my practice in Illinois. He lived with us many years through thick and lots of thin. He raised all of my children. However, he was particularly needed for my oldest son Kris, who is now deceased.)

Our Friend, "Charcoal"

Dear Charcoal, This letter is to thank you for doing such a fine job in raising a family. You came upon the scene when a little boy named Kris needed some companionship. You didn't complain, or criticize him, or tell him to eat his vegetables. He had parents for those necessary parts of growing up. You simply loved him, licked him, and snuggled up to him at night. Dad would hear Kris talking to you at night. Such conversations between little boys and kitty friends should be private. So Dad would softly close the bedroom door and go back to his room. Dad understood his job and incompletely understood your job. So Dad did what he was supposed to do for Kris. And you would do your part. Dad understood that God knew that Kris needed a Charcoal in his life to fill in the gaps that fathers could not. Who would have thought that a Havana Brown cat could be so important to such a small light here on earth in the injured heart of a little boy. Well the Boy grew up to be a fine man and went off to live his life as men do.

And you Charcoal stayed around long enough to

bring two more sons and a daughter. You even found time to help Dad through some hard spots before you went to your reward at a very ripe old age. Your message was always the same; listen, lick, and purr. Even your passing after fourteen years of a very busy life taught a small boy named John Paul a little bit about death. He would sit in the yard under the pine tree where you are buried and "wait for you to come back out of the ground when you woke up".

As time passed he understood the finality of your death in a way that only children can. Well, little boys grow up to become men and dads. And sometimes they don't live as long as we had all planned. So now, Charcoal, you are needed again in heaven to do what you do best; listen, lick and purr. Dr. Bob

The Saga of Him and Her

How the best intentions do work! This is the true story of two standard poodle puppies that are now safely tucked in to some very nice homes with people who will love them for the rest of their lives. Since homeless puppies are not always so lucky, I wanted to show you that good things can come about when good people come together with good intentions. History: These puppies entered the world in a motor home traveling through the US. There was a brief stop here where their siblings all were sold. For some unknown reason these two were left.

They found themselves in a neighborhood in Hot Springs where a kindly lady began to feed them. She was of humble means, but always found a way to feed them the best she could. After two months, she finally decided that no one other than herself was particularly interested in their future. So she took them in to a home with several other mouths to feed. She brought them to a vet clinic for vaccinations where I met her. They looked familiar to me, as I had vaccinated what I believed to be one of their brothers, whom I should call Village Lucky Puppy, in May here in the Village I was struck by their similarities in color, structure, and personality to the Village Lucky Puppy. Discussions with Kindly Lady confirmed their origin. She paid for their vaccinations and other matters and took them home

I left for the Village determined to find patrons for the puppies that she had named Him and Her, so that eventually they would respond to new names with their new homes. Day One: My first call was to a very fine person here who immediately found a loving couple for Hero.

I discouraged New Loving Pet Parents from taking both of them because two 50 lb. doggies in their lovely home would eventually lead to some disasters in the home, and an inevitable division of attentions and possibly some rivalries. So they brought her into their home. I must report that she is in a wonderful home where she is spoiled around the clock! Day Seven: I finally brought Him home with me determined to find him a home since I knew what a burden feeding an additional mouth was for Kindly Lady. Day Twelve: Time was running out. My network of Village Loving Pet Home Finders had not as yet found a suitable home. He had also begun to find his way into our home, since he was such a gentleman. Totally house-trained!!

So I contacted the Village Groomed, Bonnie

Murdoch, who immediately offered to clip him and help find a home. What a welcome asset to our Village, she and her husband Boyd are!! Him was now officially a standard poodle, complete with neckerchief and a newfound spring to his step. That day I went for my bi-monthly visit to Dr. Larsen, another pet lover, who, besides setting me straight once again, offered to assist in the search. Day Fourteen: Must find Him a home as our Friend Clifford is not a suitable partner for any puppy due to his exuberance, weight, and intact testicle apparatus. Noon, Day Fourteen. As I walked in, the phone rang. Dr Larsen, in his usual excited voice, said that he had a home for Him. (Now follow this closely). He mentioned Him to his wife, Melissa, who, of course, immediately wanted Him for their home; which is already amply supplied with kitty and doggy friends. So , while sitting at their clinic in Hot Springs, Melissa felt an urging to go next door to the groomed, Sissy, who has an office adjacent to their Hot Springs clinic. Melissa finally followed this urging, where she immediately found that a blind lady had just lost her male standard poodle to old age and was devastated by this loss. Final Day: So, fellow Villagers that is the end of the story. He is now busy filling in that loss in the heart of his new mother. Epilogue: Everything here fell into place with some providential assistance. However, many displaced puppies and kitties do not fare so well. Please find it in your hearts to assist where you can with one or more of the humane societies in this area. Give your friends a hug for me, knowing that they are safe and secure.

The Final "Point"

There comes that day when Mom and Dad realize that the "time" has come to say goodbye. Faithful Shorthair pointer. Fourteen years young, has reached that point of diminishing capacity. She hurts all of the time now. Hard to get up. The days spent sleeping between meals and the loving pats and routines in which she has played such an important part for all of these years aren't much fun anymore. Mom and Dad looked worried all of the time. They don't laugh as much. They speak in worried tones. Faithful paces the house now in discomforting patterns. Her eyesight is poor but the old smeller is still operational for the twice daily food bowl search. She had a close call about a year ago with Addisonian Crisis.

This condition is triggered by low thyroid function. She had gone into seizures and had staggered around in circles. Mom and Dad had brought her in on an emergency call. Thankfully, she had quickly responded to the treatment. Medication and a change in diet had eventually resolved the matter. So she had enjoyed another year with Mom and Dad. This morning Dad had called and asked Doc to come and pick her up. When He came, she sensed something was up. Doc took all of her things with her, since us humans can sometimes do better with no physical reminders in the home. The heart and mind are sufficient storage centers for the many fond memories that always overcome the pain and feelings of today. Time does make the memories grow fonder and the pain fade away. That is how it has always been. So Doc took her, with Dad's permission, for a last romp through the fields. A spark of times past seemed to generate a little spring into that trot, which soon turned into a canter. As Providence often provides, a bird flushed up in front of Faithful. For a moment that lady froze; the front leg came up (a little), and ... there was your perfect day!!! Dr. Bob.

"Gentle Ben"

Ben Leinum
(September 1986-March 21, 2001)

Today my heart is breaking,
Hot tears streaming down my face.
Last night my best friend left this world,
For a far better place.
His body had grown weary,
His eyesight very dim...
The strong brave heart that beat so true,
was also failing him.
I told him that I loved him,
how sad we had to part...
But that he'd always be with me,
locked deep inside my heart.
I wrapped my arms around him,
and whispered soft and low...
"I know how much you love me "Ben",
but now it's time to go."
As gently as a sunset,
fades evening into night...
God sent an angel for him,
and together they took flight.
I know the day will come sweet "Ben",
when I'll be called home too...
And as I enter Heavens' gates,
I shall look for you.
I know you will be waiting,
and as our eyes do meet...
You'll run and place your tennis ball,
down right between my feet.
Then you'll do your prancing dance,

just like you used to do...
Each time you wanted me to come,
and play a game with you.
Again my eyes will fill with tears, but not from pain
but joy...
For eternity right by my side,
my beautiful golden boy.

Love always,

Your best friend, Gretchen

32950906R00087

Made in the USA
Charleston, SC
30 August 2014